Everyman, I will go with thee,
and be thy guide

Miguel de Cervantes

EIGHT INTERLUDES

Translated and Edited by
DAWN L. SMITH
Trent University, Canada

Consultant Editor for this volume
MELVEENA MCKENDRICK
University of Cambridge

EVERYMAN
J. M. DENT · LONDON
CHARLES E. TUTTLE
VERMONT

J. M. Dent
Orion Publishing Group
Orion House, 5 Upper St Martin's Lane,
London WC2H 9EA
and
Charles E. Tuttle Co., Inc.
28 South Main Street,
Rutland, Vermont 05701, USA

Typeset in Sabon by CentraCet Ltd, Cambridge
Printed in Great Britain by
The Guernsey Press Co. Ltd, Guernsey, C.I.

British Library Cataloguing-in-Publication Data
is available upon request.

ISBN 0 460 87751 8

To the
memory of my father,
DONALD BANKS (1891–1975),
whose love for language
and interest in Spain are an
enduring inspiration

CONTENTS

NOTE ON THE AUTHOR AND EDITOR

MIGUEL DE CERVANTES was born in Alcalá de Henares in 1547 to relatively humble parents. Little is known of his early years. In 1569 he enlisted in Italy as a soldier under the command of Don Juan of Austria and took part in the battle of Lepanto against the Turks (1571), where he was severely wounded. On his way back to Spain in 1575, he was captured by corsairs and imprisoned in Algiers for five years. After he was ransomed in 1580, he returned to Madrid. In 1584 he married Catalina de Salazar. Appointed king's commissary in 1587, he went to Andalusia to gather provisions for the Armada against England. In 1594 he became a tax collector for the same region and was briefly imprisoned in Seville, charged with financial impropriety. He moved with his family to Valladolid in 1604. Upon his return to Madrid in 1606 he entered his most active period of literary activity, which lasted until his death in Madrid in 1616.

Published First Part of *La Galatea* (a pastoral novel) in 1585; First Part of *Don Quixote* (1605); *Novelas ejemplares* (*Exemplary Novels*) (1613); *El viaje del Parnaso* (*The Journey to Parnassus*) and the *Adjunta al Parnaso* (*Postscript to Parnassus*) (1614); *Ocho comedias y ocho entremeses* (*Eight Plays and Eight Interludes*) and Second Part of *Don Quixote* (1615); *Los trabajos de Persiles y Segismunda* (*The Trials of Persiles and Segismunda*) (1617).

DAWN SMITH is Professor Emeritus at Trent University, Ontario, Canada. She has written extensively on Golden Age drama and performance.

CHRONOLOGY OF CERVANTES'S LIFE

Year	Age	Life
1547		Born in Alcalá de Henares, near Madrid, 29 September (?) to Rodrigo de Cervantes and Leonor de Cortinas
1551	4	Family moves to Valladolid
1552	5	Rodrigo de Cervantes is imprisoned for debts
1553	6	Family moves to Córdoba
1564	17	(?) Family in Seville
1566	19	Family moves to Madrid
1568	21	(?) Cervantes studies with Juan López de Hoyos in Madrid

CHRONOLOGY OF HIS TIMES

Year	Literary and Artistic Context	Historical Events
1547	1st *Index* of prohibited books in Spain	Deaths of Francis I of France and Henry VIII of England
1554	*Lazarillo de Tormes* published in Madrid	Spanish prince Philip marries Mary Tudor in Winchester Cathedral
1556		Emperor Charles V abdicates His son becomes Philip II of Spain Death of Ignatius Loyola
1558		Deaths of Charles V and Mary Tudor Elizabeth I becomes queen of England
1559	Jorge de Montemayor, *La Diana*	Death of Henri II of France Philip II marries Isabel of Valois
1560	Geneva Bible published	
1561	Births of Francis Bacon and Spanish poet Luis de Góngora	The Spanish court is established in Madrid
1562	Birth of Lope de Vega	End of Council of Trent (established in 1545)
1563		Building starts on El Escorial palace outside Madrid
1564	Births of Shakespeare, Christopher Marlowe and Galileo	
1566		Revolt in the Netherlands
1567	Lope de Rueda, *Los pasos*	
1568		Moriscos revolt in southern Spain Death of Don Carlos, son of Philip II of Spain

Year	Age	Life
1569	22	Travels to Rome
		(?) Joins household of Monsignor Acquaviva
1570	23	Enlists in Spanish army at Naples
1571	24	Wounded at the Battle of Lepanto
1573	26	Takes part in a military expedition against Tunis
1575	28	Captured by Barbary pirates and imprisoned in Algiers
1576	29	Tries to escape from prison
1577	30	Second attempted escape
		His brother Rodrigo is ransomed
1578	31	Third attempted escape
1579	32	Fourth attempted escape
1580	33	Ransomed by Trinitarian monks
		Returns to Madrid
1581	34	Travels to Portugal with Philip II's entourage
1582	35	(?) Writes *Life in Algiers*
1584	37	12 December: marries Catalina de Salazar in Esquivias (near Toledo)
		Isabel de Saavedra born
1585	38	*La Galatea* (Part I) published
		Death of Cervantes's father
		Miguel sells two plays (both now lost)
1587	40	Appointed king's commissary in Andalusia, responsible for provisioning the Armada against England
1590	43	Unsuccessfully petitions Council of the Indies for post in the Indies
		Adds Saavedra to surname

Year	Literary and Artistic Context	Historical Events
1571		Formation of Holy League against Turks
		Battle of Lepanto
1572	Luis de Camoens, *Los Lusiadas*	Massacre of St Bartholomew
1576	James Burbage builds the Theatre in London	
	Blackfriars Theatre opens	
	Death of Titian	
1577	El Greco settles in Toledo	
	Birth of Rubens	
1578		Death of Don Juan of Austria
		Death of King Sebastian of Portugal in battle of Alcazarquivir
1579	1st permanent theatre in Madrid, the Corral de la Cruz, opens	
1580	Montaigne, *Essays*	Philip II becomes king of Portugal
	Death of Luis de Camoens	
1581		
1582		Death of St Teresa of Avila
1583	Juan de la Cueva, *Comedias y tragedias*	Sir Walter Raleigh's expedition to Virginia
1584	Palladio builds Teatro Olimpico in Vicenza	Assassination of William of Orange
		Philip II moves into El Escorial
1585	St John of the Cross, *Cántico espiritual*	
	Death of Ronsard	
1587	Christopher Marlowe, *Tamburlaine the Great*	
1588	El Greco, *Burial of the Count of Orgaz*	Defeat of Spanish Armada
1589	St Teresa, *Works*	

Year	Age	Life
1592	45	Charged with fraud, he is briefly jailed, but later cleared
		Signs contract to write six plays at fifty ducats apiece
1593	46	Death of Cervantes's mother
1594	47	Cervantes is briefly in Madrid, then returns to Andalusia as a tax collector
1595	48	Wins first prize in a poetry contest in Zaragoza, in honour of the canonisation of San Jacinto
1597	50	Spends several months in prison in Seville, accused of failure to settle accounts
1604	57	Cervantes and his family move to Valladolid
		He finishes writing *Don Quixote* (Part I)
1605	58	*Don Quixote* (Part I) published
1606	59	Cervantes and family return to Madrid
1612	65	Thomas Shelton publishes the first English translation of *Don Quixote* in London
1613	66	*The Exemplary Novels* published
		Cervantes becomes a member of the Third Order of San Francisco
1614	67	*The Journey to Parnassus* published
		The 'false' *Don Quixote* II appears, under the name of Alfonso Fernández de Avellaneda
		The first French translation of *Don Quixote*, by Césare Oudin, published in Paris

Year	Literary and Artistic Context	Historical Events
1592	Death of Montaigne.	
1595		Accession of Henri IV of France
1596		The English fleet sacks Cadiz
1598	Birth of Zurbarán Lope de Vega, *La Arcadia*	Death of Philip II Accession of Philip III
1599	Birth of Velázquez Mateo Alemán, *Guzmán de Alfarache, I* The Globe playhouse opens in London Death of Edmund Spenser	
1600	Birth of Calderón de la Barca	
1601	(?) 1st performance of *Hamlet*	Philip III of Spain moves capital to Valladolid (until 1606)
1603	Lope de Vega, 1st volume of Collected Plays *Hamlet* (1st quarto) published	Death of Elizabeth I James I king of England and Scotland
1605	Ben Jonson, *Volpone* (?) 1st performance of *King Lear*	
1606		Virginia Company founded
1611	(?) 1st performance of *The Tempest*	
1613	(?) John Webster, *The Duchess of Malfi* The Globe Theatre destroyed by fire	

Year	Age	Life
1615	68	Cervantes publishes *Don Quixote II* and *Eight Plays and Eight Interludes*
1616	69	Cervantes finishes writing *The Trials of Persiles and Sigismunda*
		23 April: death of Cervantes in Madrid
		Buried in the Convent of Trinitarian nuns near by
1617		*The Trials of Persiles and Sigismunda* published

Year	Literary and Artistic Context	Historical Events
1616	Death of Shakespeare	

INTRODUCTION

Cervantes and His Time

Miguel de Cervantes was born half-way through the sixteenth century and lived into the second decade of the seventeenth century. This was a remarkably long life for the time and it spanned one of the most extraordinary periods in Spanish history. In 1547, the year that Cervantes was born, Charles I was king of Spain, as well as head of the Holy Roman Empire (which gave him the title of Emperor Charles V). The country was still riding high on the euphoria of conquest and discovery in the New World initiated by Christopher Columbus in 1492, although the price of such triumphs would be apparent by the end of Cervantes's life. Other events of 1492 still threw long shadows that reached into every aspect of Spanish life: among these were the repercussions from the conquest of the last Moorish kingdom of Granada and the expulsion of more than one hundred thousand Spanish Jews that same fateful year.[1]

Despite the fact that Spain was now the most powerful and feared nation in Europe, the bright expectations and optimistic mood engendered by almost six decades of expansion and largely illusory prosperity were already dimming. When Cervantes was nine years old, the world-weary king/emperor abdicated and retired to the monastery at Yuste, where he died two years later.

He was succeeded by his son, Philip II, whose long reign ended just two years short of the turn of the century. During that time Spain was involved in costly wars against the Turks and their allies in the Mediterranean, as well as against enemies from the North, especially the English, whose ships challenged Spain's claim to mastery of the seas. In 1571, the threat from the Ottoman empire was decisively ended when the allied forces of Venice, the papacy and Spain fought and won the Battle of Lepanto. Against the English, Spain was less successful: in 1588 the Spanish fleet was largely destroyed in its disastrous encounter in the English Channel with a small force commanded by Sir Francis Drake.

Cervantes grew up in the shadow of these larger events; but much of the biographical evidence is sketchy, if not purely conjectural. What is known for certain is that he was born in Alcalá de Henares, close to Madrid, the third child of an impoverished middle-class family. His mother, Leonor de Cortinas, came from a family of modest rural landowners, who evidently considered that she had married beneath her. His father, Rodrigo de Cervantes, was a not very successful barber-surgeon who seems virtually to have abandoned his family when his son Miguel was still young.[2] At some point the family followed Rodrigo to Andalusia; it is believed that they took up residence in Seville when Miguel was seventeen, and that they returned to Madrid two years later. Little is known about Cervantes's schooling, although he may have studied with a schoolmaster in Madrid by the name of López de Hoyos.[3] Any further education of a formal nature may have been curtailed by an indiscretion that seems to have obliged him to leave the capital in a hurry.[4] Once again, there is little hard evidence and this must be supplemented by oblique references in Cervantes's later writings. Nevertheless, it is certain that by 1569 the young man was in Rome, apparently in the service of an Italian prelate called Monsignor Acquaviva. By 1571 he and his brother Rodrigo had enlisted in the Spanish army in Naples. In August 1571 an alliance against the Turks was formed between Spain, Venice and the papacy. The military forces of this so-called Holy League were commanded by the legendary Don Juan of Austria, illegitimate brother of Philip II. In October the Christian and Turkish fleets confronted each other in the Gulf of Lepanto and fought a terrible battle. Although the Christians won, it was a costly victory. Among the casualties was Miguel de Cervantes, who lost the use of his left hand as a result of wounds.

In 1575, after participating in other military campaigns under Don Juan, Cervantes and his brother embarked for Spain. Unfortunately, the ship in which they were travelling was captured by corsairs from North Africa and the course of Cervantes's life was abruptly changed. He spent the next five years in captivity in Algiers while his impoverished family tried to raise the money to free the two brothers. The sum required for Miguel's release was unusually high because the letters of recommendation he was carrying from his former commanders led his captors to believe that he was someone of importance. Rodrigo was finally released in 1577, but Miguel spent another three years in captivity. During that time he attempted to escape at least four times. How he managed to survive these transgressions without severe punishment is a mystery that has continued to intrigue scholars. On the other hand, it is unarguable that his adventures in Algiers provided him with material which would later bring an unusual perspective to his writing, both as novelist and playwright.

The Spain that Cervantes returned to in 1580 was much changed from the Spain he had left ten years before. Without money or patrons, his life seems henceforth to have been plagued with debt and financial anxiety, as well as with frustration in his attempts to secure better employment. In 1584 he married Catalina de Salazar, a woman who was much younger than he was, but this union did little to improve his financial standing; nor, apparently, did it bring him much happiness – not, at least, until later in life. The couple remained childless, although it is generally thought that a daughter, Isabel, was born of Cervantes's liaison with a young married woman called Ana Franca. Many years later, after her mother's death, Isabel entered the service of Miguel's sister Magdalena; a contemporary document refers to her as Isabel de Saavedra – the name that Cervantes added to his own surname around 1590.

Cervantes spent little time with his wife during the next sixteen years. Employed as a king's commissary, he was charged with requisitioning provisions for the Armada that would sail against England. For seven years he travelled up and down Andalusia, carrying out this thankless task for which he received little pay, or only the promise of future remuneration. The towns he visited scarcely had enough for themselves and were understandably reluctant to part with their precious oil and corn in return for the dubious expectation of eventual payment. Cervantes aroused such hostility, in fact, that he was twice excommunicated for appropriating Church property and even spent a brief spell in prison, apparently on an unsubstantiated charge of cooking the accounts. He did not fare much better during the following years, during which he served as a tax collector – a job that took him back to Andalusia, but did nothing to improve either his finances or his popularity with the local population. In 1597 he was charged with failing to deliver tax money. This was a serious and complicated charge; since Cervantes was unable to raise the necessary funds to post a bond, he was imprisoned in Seville for some months. During this time he may have begun to write *Don Quixote*.

With the beginning of the new century Cervantes and his family settled briefly in Valladolid, the city to which the new king, Philip III, briefly moved his court. Cervantes was now in his fifties, without much prospect of changing his fortunes; yet the remaining twelve years of his life proved to be his most productive period as a writer: the First Part of *Don Quixote* was published in 1605, followed by *The Exemplary Novels* (1613), *The Journey to Parnassus* (1614), *Eight Plays and Eight Interludes* and the Second Part of *Don Quixote* in 1615. *The Trials of Persiles and Sigismunda* was published posthumously in 1617. This was a truly astonishing achievement, all the more remarkable considering that before 1605 he had apparently produced no more than a pastoral romance (*The Galatea*), several undated plays and a number of elegiac or eulogistic poems. It may be that some of his later work had previously existed in outline or rough draft, but that he waited until he had leisure at his disposal before he decided to revise and polish them for publication.

Cervantes's life oscillated between two poles, which he himself characterised in *Don Quixote* as Arms versus Letters ('Armas y Letras').[5] As a young man he gave himself eagerly to the pursuit of Arms and paid dearly for his choice, both at Lepanto and in his years of captivity in Algiers. When he sought fame with his pen later in life, the material rewards were also disappointing, despite the popular success of *Don Quixote* during his lifetime.

The Spanish writer and philosopher, Julián Marías, attributes Cervantes's originality to the fact that, unlike contemporaries such as Lope de Vega, Quevedo or Góngora, he viewed life from the margin, not from the centre of intellectual and court life.[6] This perspective allowed him to speak with a detachment that is often refreshingly iconoclastic. From the margin, too, come the characters of *Don Quixote*, of the *Exemplary Tales* and *The Interludes*, drawn from the people Cervantes encountered on his many travels: in Italy, in Philip II's navy at Lepanto, in the dungeons of Algiers, along the dusty roads and in the bustling inns of Castile, his portrayal of the underside of urban life in Seville and Madrid has an authenticity that can only come from personal experience.

Cervantes spent the last years of his life in Madrid, beset to the end by financial vexations and personal losses. He died on 23 April 1616. In one of history's accidents, his death coincided almost to the day with that of his great contemporary, William Shakespeare.[7]

The Rise of the Public Theatre in Spain

It was not until the 1580s that theatre in Spain acquired a measure of stability and a clearly defined place in urban society. This came about with the establishment of permanent commercial playhouses in Madrid and other major cities.[8] Earlier in the century the average Spaniard's experience of theatre came from religious performances in the street and public square. Drama played an important part in the festivities organised by the trade guilds to celebrate the great religious holidays at Christmas, Easter and Corpus Christi. As well as processions, which included elaborate floats ('carretas'), there were one-act morality plays ('autos sacramentales') performed on carts or raised platforms. The Jesuit colleges also made use of drama as an instrument of moral persuasion and instruction, not only for the edification of their own pupils, but also for a wider audience. These plays were mostly written in Latin, but as a concession to the lay public they began to include scenes in the vernacular.

Secular drama was restricted to private, aristocratic and royal patrons until the middle of the sixteenth century, when groups of travelling players popularised theatre by performing in towns and villages throughout the country.[9] Their repertoire included plays of their own invention, largely devised from existing sources; they were also influenced by Italian drama, particularly the *commedia dell'arte*, which was brought to Spain around 1550 by companies of itinerant Italian players. The best-remembered of the early Spanish actor-managers is Lope de Rueda, who seems to have been active from the early 1540s until his death some twenty-five years later. Besides his reputation as an actor, he is also known as the writer of plays and comic sketches. In the Prologue to his *Eight Plays and Eight Interludes*, Cervantes recalls that as a young man he saw Rueda perform. His admiration for him as an actor is evident, even as he recalls the primitive conditions of both stage and performance.

The first permanent theatres opened in Madrid (the Corral de la Cruz in 1579 and the Corral del Príncipe in 1583); others soon followed in major cities throughout the country.[10] Earlier playwrights, such as Lope de Rueda, Juan del Encina and Gil Vicente, had fallen out of fashion; their place was taken by new writers like Juan de la Cueva (in Seville), Cristóbal de Virués (in Valencia) and Lupercio Leonardo de Argensola (in Zaragoza). There was a swing to classical tragedy, reflecting a revival of interest throughout Europe in the drama of Seneca and further influenced, it is thought, by the recent translation of Aristotle's *Poetics* into Italian.[11] The plays written in Spain in this period often run to four or five acts, the language is rhetorical and erudite, the plots turgid and, by modern standards, melodramatic.

Cervantes As Playwright

Cervantes claims to have written 'twenty or thirty plays' during the decade following his return from captivity in Algiers. The dates of composition and the titles of most of these plays are unknown. Of the three specifically mentioned in the Prologue to *Eight Plays and Eight Interludes*, only two survive today: *Life in Algiers* (*El trato de Argel*) and *The Siege of Numantia* (*La destrucción de Numancia*).[12] The first is a vivid, if episodic account of Cervantes's experiences as a captive in North Africa.

The second is an account of the heroic defence of the Celtiberian city Numantia by its citizens against the invading Romans in 133 BC. The story was already a national legend, extolling the bravery of the Numantians, who preferred to die rather than surrender to their conquerors. Its patriotic theme clearly appealed to Cervantes, who had fought for his country at Lepanto. No doubt the play also stirred those first audiences, as it has continued to stir Spanish audiences at times of national crisis, even as recently as 1936.[13]

Almost three decades later, Cervantes looked back on that fleeting period of success and recalled that 'with other things to occupy my time, I put aside my pen and wrote no more plays'. This no doubt is an allusion to the long period when he was employed in government service in Andalusia. During this time the theatre was undergoing further changes which henceforth would define it as a commercial enterprise, dependent on the laws of supply and demand. Actors responded to these changes by establishing powerful professional companies.[14] By the time Cervantes was ready to take up his 'former leisurely way of life' and, recalling his previous successes, attempted to sell some new plays, he found to his chagrin that his work was no longer considered good box-office. Since no actor-manager would accept his plays, he was obliged to sell them to a bookseller for publication.

Was this another example of Cervantes's bad luck, or had time simply passed him by? Certainly, the old style of plays to which he had subscribed was now out of fashion, supplanted by the New Comedy ('Comedia nueva') under its presiding genius, Lope de Vega. Cervantes himself wrote in his 1615 Prologue: 'Along came great Lope de Vega, one of nature's prodigies, and made off with the theatrical crown.'

There are a number of indications that the strained relationship between the two men went beyond mere professional jealousy. Jean Canavaggio gives the details of slighting remarks on both sides.[15] In the Prologue to the spurious Second Part of *Don Quixote* the mysterious author, Alonso Fernández de Avellaneda, writes scornfully of Cervantes and accuses him of insulting Lope.[16] To this attack Cervantes replies in the Prologue to his own Second Part, alleging that 'I revere that man's genius, and admire his works and his virtuous and unceasing industry.' Finally, in the *Postscript to Parnassus*, Cervantes refers to an incident that had occurred when he was living in Valladolid, and that obviously still causes him pain: his niece had accepted – and paid for – delivery of a sonnet, 'badly written, lacklustre, with no wit or appeal whatever, insulting *Don Quixote* ...' There is good reason to believe that this refers to a crude and vulgar poem written either by Lope or at his direction, cruelly ridiculing both *Don Quixote* and its author.[17]

Beyond these personal attacks (which were not unusual in literary circles at the time), it is possible that Lope was more directly involved in blocking Cervantes's return to the theatre after 1600.[18] In the Prologue to *Eight Plays and Eight Interludes* Cervantes notes that when Lope 'made off with the theatrical crown ... *all the actors became his slaves and were subject to his rule*' (my emphasis). This suggests that, at the very least, members of the theatrical establishment were reluctant to offend the influential Lope. Perhaps, too, they considered that Cervantes's plays were risky investments for a public infatuated with the made-to-measure plots of the new style.

Cervantes does not conceal his contempt for those actor-managers who refused even to look at his plays.[19] In the Dedication to his patron, the Count of Lemos, which also accompanies the 1615 edition, Cervantes returns to the subject:

> ... these plays and interludes [are] not so lacking in flavour, it seems to me, that they cannot please someone; in their favour, it must be said that they have never been handled or staged in the theatre, thanks to the extreme caution of the actors ['farsantes'], who are only interested in masterpieces by established authors ['obras grandes y de graves autores'], even though they are sometimes proven wrong.

Canavaggio suggests that several actor-managers who had previously staged Cervantes's plays either died or retired from the theatre around 1610.[20] Furthermore, beyond his quarrel with timid actor-managers and bickering actors (whom he also attacks in the Prologue), there seems to lie a deeper disillusionment. Already, in the First Part of *Don Quixote*, in a discussion between the Canon and the priest, the latter had complained that plays had become a marketable commodity ('mercadería vendible').[21] The speaker blames the actor-managers for debasing the theatre and goes out of his way to exonerate the poets (particularly 'one most fertile genius of these kingdoms' – i.e. Lope de Vega). Despite these honeyed words, it may be that by 1615, after attempting in vain to have his plays performed, Cervantes came to regard his rival with less charity.

The Origin and Evolution of Interludes in Spain

The Spanish word for interlude is 'entremés', derived from the Latin 'intermedium' ('in the middle of'). In sixteenth- and seventeenth-century Castile it appears to have been used primarily to refer to a dramatic Interlude (although, through the influence of French, it may also have been used to refer to food served between main courses).[22] Covarrubias's dictionary defines the word as 'a comic and witty performance, set between the acts of a play, for the purpose of pleasing and entertaining

the audience'. While the 'entremés' probably resembled the
farces and Interludes popular elsewhere in Europe (notably in
France, Germany and England) during the late Middle Ages and
early Renaissance,[23] it soon developed characteristics that
reflected Spanish tastes and experiences.

Although the plays of the early writer, Juan del Encina
(1468–1529), contain scenes that are obviously intended to
provide comic relief, only later were the terms 'entremés' and
'paso' used to denote such scenes as separate Interludes.[24] Lope
de Rueda is now generally credited with giving them more
cohesiveness and independence. Los pasos (published in 1567)
were a great popular success, largely because Rueda himself was
a talented actor and a shrewd manager. As a writer, he created
lively comic dialogue in prose; his characters and situations
draw freely from traditional rustic farce, to which are added
figures, such as the braggart soldier and the cuckolded old man,
that are familiar stock-in-trade in commedia dell'arte, with
antecedents in the Roman comedies of Plautus.[25]

After 1600 the Interlude entered a new phase in its development in Spain, no doubt as a reflection of the popularity of New
Comedy and the close relationship between the two types of
theatre. Lope de Vega himself wrote a number of Interludes,
using verse instead of prose: a practice that soon became the
general rule.

Emphasis shifted from the predominantly rustic and carnival-
esque world portrayed by Lope de Rueda to include characters
familiar to an urban audience: foolish or dishonest doctors,
lawyers and officials, flatterers and rogues, braggarts and cowards – all the panoply of human folly and intrigue encountered
in the newly burgeoning cities, of which Madrid and Seville
were the foremost examples. The plot is often little more than a
succession of characters who engage in verbal and gestural
sparring until tension is resolved in a ritual climax of song and
dance.[26] The most prolific writer of this new type of interlude
was Luis Quiñones de Benavente (1589?–1651), while Francisco
de Quevedo (1580–1645), Lope de Vega (1562–1635) and
Calderón de la Barca (1600–1681) all contributed to what
became known as Minor theatre ('Teatro menor').

The popularity of the Interlude in the theatre of seventeenth-
century Spain is understandable for several reasons. In the first
place, it became an indispensable part of the theatrical event: a

normal afternoon's performance in a *Corral de Comedias* consisted of a three-act play, with an Interlude inserted between each of the acts.[27] This answered a number of purposes: given the disparate composition of the audience and its restless nature, Interludes provided light relief from the main action; they also distracted the audience's attention while necessary changes were made to costume and scenery in preparation for the ensuing acts; at times, Interludes might even be counted on to rescue a performance from failure.[28]

Interludes followed a formula that was no doubt recognised and expected by the audience. While they tapped into well-known traditions (such as ballad literature, carnival customs, the picaresque novel), their appeal also depended on their comfortable familiarity. This is a world of low comedy, of ordinary people contending with everyday problems (involving money, hunger, jealousy, sexual appetite) and overcoming them with a freedom not usually vouchsafed to the average citizen.[29] As Eugenio Asensio puts it, 'morals are on vacation'.

A measure of their popularity is that they were viewed with distrust by the authorities. There are disapproving references to the 'lascivious movements' ('meneos') and 'suggestive dances' that characterise them (see notes to *The Magic Cave of Salamanca* and *The Election of the Magistrates of Daganzo*). What might be considered relatively harmless as long as it remained within the bounds of mere slapstick was potentially subsersive if it strayed into satire.

At the same time, the moral dimension of the Interlude may also be asserted. It is significant, for example, that Calderón specifically wrote a series of Interludes to accompany his Corpus Christi plays (*Autos sacramentales*).[30] The relief produced by the contemplation of unheroic characters in comic, and sometimes grotesque, situations, is not unlike the effect caused by the dwarfs in the court paintings of Velázquez: the spectator is first struck by the contrast between two opposites, then led to ponder the deeper implications of the juxtaposition. For the seventeenth-century theatregoer, constantly reminded of such contrasts in sermon, art and literature, comedy was as apt a teacher as tragedy. Perhaps no one knew this better than Cervantes, who wrote in *Don Quixote*: 'To be witty and write humorously requires great genius. The cunningest part in a play is the fool's, for a man who wants to be taken for a simpleton must never be one' (II, 3).

Eight New Interludes 'Never Yet Performed'

Although there is no conclusive evidence for establishing the actual dates of composition of Cervantes's Interludes, it is generally thought that they acquired their present form after 1610. In some cases this belief is borne out by internal references to specific events (for example, in *Sir Vigilant*, *The Widowed Pimp*, *The Man Who Pretended He Was from Biscay*, and *The Marvellous Puppet Show*); however, it is possible that some of them were written earlier and revised later for publication.

In the 1615 *Prologue* Cervantes claims that, when his plays found no favour with the actor-managers, he 'put them away in a chest and condemned them to eternal silence'. Later, however, he relates that he took them out again 'along with some Interludes that I had put away as well . . .'

Certainly, six of the Interludes were in existence by 1614, the year that the *Postscript to Parnassus* was published. This curious work takes the form of a conversation between Cervantes himself and a rich young man called Pancracio de Roncesvalles, who is charged with delivering to him a letter from Apollo on the subject of Spanish poets. In the course of the rambling, humorous, and sometimes bitter conversation, Cervantes mentions that he has six plays as yet unpublished, together with six Interludes. A year later, in 1615, he published *eight* plays with an equal number of Interludes. Perhaps the publisher, Juan de Villarroel, insisted that the original number be increased, on the grounds that this would make the volume more saleable.

In later years other Interludes have been attributed to Cervantes, in particular, *The Chatterboxes* (*Los habladores*), *Tthe Prison in Seville* (*La cárcel de Sevilla*) and *The Hospital for the Dying* (*El hospital de los podridos*); however, in style and characterisation these pieces are clearly inferior to the Interludes known to be by Cervantes, and their attribution is now generally discounted.

Indications as to what Cervantes thought about the Interlude as a dramatic genre appear in allusions throughout his written work. In the Exemplary Novel called *The Dogs' Colloquy* (*El coloquio de los perros*) he gives a vivid description of the kind of rambunctious, knockabout scenes that were typical in the time of Lope de Rueda. The dog Berganza tells his companion of his adventures when he joined a company of actors and became 'a great performer of Interludes and dumbshows':

> They [the actors] put a fringed muzzle on me and taught me to attack anyone in the theatre they picked on; since it's the custom for Interludes to end in beatings, in our Company they used to whistle me out and I'd knock everyone over and trample on them. This caused a lot of amusement among those who didn't know what was going on and my master made a lot of money out of it.

In the play *The Grand Sultana*, a musician speaks approvingly of the merry dances and songs that he has seen performed in the theatre in Spain. He claims that they entertained and cheered the audience 'more than any Interlude about a hungry man, a thief or the victim of a beating'. It is significant, perhaps, that Cervantes himself avoids such crudely stock characters in his own Interludes. Nor does he end his plays with beatings and uproar. Except for *The Marvellous Puppet Show*, in which the implied fracas between the quartermaster and the townspeople takes place off stage, all the other Interludes end with songs and dancing.

If a common theme emerges from these scattered allusions, it is that Cervantes believed that some characteristics of the Interlude as he knew it were in need of change. In his usual fashion, he applied his ideas in eight 'new' Interludes.

As we have seen, Cervantes set out to explain in the Prologue why these Interludes and the plays for which they were written were 'never yet performed', and why he subsequently made them available in published form. The reasons he gives, however, are a long way from being conclusive. Recently, some critics have argued that when Cervantes found that no one would produce his plays in the theatre, he made a deliberate decision to redirect them to a *reading* public.[31]

This theory appears to be supported by the passage in the *Postscript to Parnassus* in which the narrator Cervantes responds to Pancracio's comment that the actor-managers must surely not know of the existence of his (six) Interludes:

Of course they know about them; but since they're satisfied with
the work of their own cronies, they won't bother taking a risk.
However, I'm planning to have my plays published so that what
flashes by – is hidden, or not understood when it's acted on the
stage, – can be contemplated at leisure. For plays are like songs:
they have their seasons and their times to be in fashion.

It is further argued that by choosing to publish his plays
Cervantes effectively directs them to a different audience, thereby
bypassing the ignorant majority (the 'vulgo') that frequented the
theatre, as well as the need to deal with peevish actors and
managers. The difficulty with this theory is that there is insufficient evidence to show which factors were causes and which
were effects; did the actor-managers think that Cervantes's Plays
and Interludes were too innovative (and therefore too risky), or
were they reacting as a claque (as Cervantes himself hints) and
taking their cue from Lope de Vega? If, in fact, Cervantes did
revise his plays subsequently for publication (although he never
actually says that he did), what was the nature of the revisions?
Are some of the Interludes more 'revised' than others and, if so,
which ones? Although Cervantes was enormously productive
during this period, his health was not good. It seems unlikely that
he would have had either the time or the inclination to make
extensive revisions to the existing Plays and Interludes, besides
adding two more of each, in little more than a year.

Perhaps the fate of *The Eight Plays and Eight Interludes* owes
more to circumstances than to intention – as was so often the
case in Cervantes's life. It is clear from the Prologue that he
originally intended them for performance and that he first
responded to their rejection by putting them away and forgetting
about them. Later, however, he was reminded of their existence
when a bookseller commented that he would have bought them
if a licensed actor-manager had not spoken disparagingly about
Cervantes's poetry. That criticism seems to have stung him into
selling the manuscript.[32]

It was quite usual for playwrights to publish their plays not
only for profit, but also in order to retain some control over
their work and to ensure that an 'authorised' version would
remain for posterity.[33] Plays by Lope de Vega first appeared in
print in 1603 and thereafter at regular intervals. The Fourth
Part of Lope's published plays came out in 1614, the year that

Cervantes announced his intention to publish his own plays. Perhaps he was encouraged by Lope's success with the reading public, or, following the acclaim for the First Part of *Don Quixote*, hoped to find similar favour for his plays.

What is different about the publication of these particular Plays and Interludes is that, contrary to the general rule, *they had not previously been performed*. In *The Postscript to Parnassus* Cervantes appears to be aware of the unusual circumstances when he justifies his intention to publish them so that they 'can be contemplated at leisure'. Certainly he would have been aware of the opportunities this offered him as a writer. Although the reading public only represented about twenty-five per cent of the total population, the market for published versions of plays was a good source of income for an impecunious playwright.[34]

By choosing to direct these plays to a reading public, did Cervantes somehow change them so drastically that they could no longer be considered suitable material for performance? Recently critics have tended to over-emphasise the novelistic characteristics of these works while apparently forgetting the equally persuasive counterclaim that Cervantes was given to *theatricalising* his novels.[35]

Cervantes, I believe, wrote his Plays and Interludes over a number of years with the initial intention that they would be performed and always from a *theatrical* point of view.[36] At the time that he decided to sell them to a bookseller it would appear that *he had no other option*; he may, therefore, have been influenced by practical considerations as much as by aesthetic ones. While he makes it clear that he added two plays and two Interludes at this stage, we do not know which were the additions, nor what revisions he made, if any. It is even possible that the existing texts were already quite suitable for readers; in fact, this may have been part of the reason why the actor-managers rejected them in the first place. Although there is no doubt that they benefit from a leisurely reading, with the opportunity for reflection, that is also true of many play texts, from Shakespeare to Tom Stoppard. It is not in itself a reason to decide that this same text is 'unperformable'.

A dramatic Interlude, by definition, is designed to be played with a longer play, to act as a foil to the action of its more substantial companion. In the case of Cervantes's Interludes, their relationship to each other was almost certainly of less importance than their relationship to the full-length plays published in the same volume. It is significant that the title page of the 1615 edition refers specifically to 'these eight plays and *their* interludes' (my emphasis). However, Cervantes gives no indication of which pieces he intended to be performed together; even the order in which they appear in print is no guide – the Plays form one discrete group, followed by the Interludes as another. Perhaps Cervantes meant them to be interchangeable, like those pictures of faces that come with a set of alternate parts and allow you to compose and recompose a number of different portraits.

To regard these Interludes as isolated units (a view that is, unfortunately, compounded by modern theatrical practices) is to remove them from their proper context. They acquire an additional, and often quite different, perspective when considered within the framework of a surrounding play. From the audience's point of view this perspective may serve to underline, or even to subvert, a theme in the longer work by re-presenting it in the Interlude in the form of low comedy. Cory A. Reed argues that the Interludes may, in fact, have been too *subversive* for contemporary audiences and that this may have been a further reason for their rejection. He also suggests that their open-endedness would have made it difficult for the audience to return to the world of the full-length play.[37]

Like their companion Plays, the Interludes also appear to engage the new style of playwriting championed by Lope de Vega and his followers. One critic suggests that Cervantes achieves this by subtly subverting the characteristics and values of the New Comedy.[38] Perhaps the best example of this occurs in the play *The Comedy of Entertainment* (*La entretenida*), which revolves around two parallel plots, one concerning the 'upstairs' world of the aristocracy, the other, the 'downstairs' world of the servants. In the third act the servants present an Interlude making fun of their masters' romantic intrigues; this ends in disarray with an abrupt return to the reality in which no one manages to get married (an obvious parody of the Lopean formula for New Comedy, according to which 'everything ends in marriage').[39]

Jean Canavaggio was one of the first to suggest that Cervantes was ahead of his time as a playwright.[40] What he wrote for the stage in the early 1600s did not easily fit into the expectations of his contemporaries (and for reasons that we have discussed, the actor-managers were evidently not prepared to take the financial risk of trying to persuade the public to change its tastes). Paradoxically, what Cervantes undoubtedly viewed as a setback would ultimately have unexpected consequences. Many features of his plays, misunderstood in the seventeenth century, have become commonplace in twentieth-century theatre: the metatheatrical interplay between fiction and reality anticipates Pirandello, and an experimental approach to *mise-en-scène* would later be championed by Bertolt Brecht. Cervantes's sharp perception of the idiosyncrasies of human behaviour and his ability to create memorable characters and lively dialogue are also qualities that transfer well to the modern stage. Scholars and theatre directors are taking a new look at these neglected Plays and Interludes and finding them to be surprisingly innovative and experimental. They may finally take the place Cervantes intended for them: in the theatre.

DAWN SMITH

References

1. For background reading to the period, see J. H. Elliott, 'Monarchy and Empire (1474–1700)'; also, J. Lynch, *Spain under the Habsburgs*.

2. Jean Canavaggio speculates that Rodrigo's modest profession 'at the bottom of the medical hierarchy' may have been a subject of some embarrassment in the family (*Cervantes*, p. 22). A barber-surgeon is one of the plaintiffs satirised in *The Divorce Court Judge*.

3. Fuller details of this and other aspects of Cervantes's life are given in the excellent biographies by Jean Canavaggio (1990) and Melveena McKendrick (1980).

4. A document discovered in the nineteenth century attests that in 1569 a warrant was issued for the arrest of a student called Miguel de Cervantes. He was accused of wounding one Antonio de Sigura, a master mason, and condemned *in absentia* to lose his right hand and to be exiled for ten years (Canavaggio, *Cervantes*, p. 46).

5. *Don Quixote* I, 37–8.

6. *Cervantes clave española* (Madrid: Alianza, 1990).

7. According to the modern Gregorian Calendar, Shakespeare's death also occurred on 23 April 1616. However, since England at that time still followed the Old Style calendar (whereas Spain had already changed to the Gregorian Calendar), Shakespeare, in fact, died ten days later.

8. For background reading, see Melveena McKendrick, *Theatre in Spain, 1490–1700*; also N. D. Shergold, *A History of the Spanish Stage from Medieval Times until the End of the Seventeenth Century*.

9. McKendrick, *Theatre in Spain*, p. 42.

10. See *Teatros del Siglo de Oro: Corrales y Coliseos en la Península Ibérica*, ed. J. M. Díez Borque (Madrid: Ministerio de Cultura [*Cuadernos de teatro clásico* 6], 1991).

11. McKendrick, *Theatre in Spain*, p. 57.

12. In *The Postscript to Parnassus* Cervantes names a further seven or eight plays (some of which may have appeared subsequently under different titles); he also claims to have written 'many more that I've forgotten'.

13. McKendrick, *Theatre in Spain*, p. 63.

14. Canavaggio, *Cervantes*, pp. 201–202.

15. *Cervantes*, pp. 203–204.

16. Published in 1614 with the title *Segundo tomo del ingenioso hidalgo Don Quijote de la Mancha, que contiene su tercera salida* (*The Second Part of the Exploits of Don Quixote of the Mancha, being the account of his third sally*), this curious work obviously aimed to capitalise on the popular success of the First Part of *Don Quixote*. Whether or not Cervantes knew the author's true identity, he reacted strongly to the book in his own Second Part (published in 1615). Cervantes actually introduces a character from Avellaneda's book in order to have him testify before a judge that Don Quixote and Sancho Panza bear no resemblance to the characters of the same name whom he had known in the 'other' *Don Quixote* (*Don Quixote* II, 72)!

17. Canavaggio, *Cervantes*, pp. 228–9.

18. McKendrick, *Cervantes*, pp. 195–201.

19. See the Prologue to *Eight Plays and Eight Interludes*.

20. *Cervantes*, p. 268.

21. *Don Quixote* I, 48.

22. According to Corominas, *Breve diccionario etimológico de la lengua castellana* (Madrid: Gredos, 1967), this usage was probably introduced through Catalan, if not directly from French. Curiously, neither *Covarrubias* (1611) nor the *Diccionario de Autoridades* (1732) mentions this meaning.

23. For a wider discussion of European Interludes, see Allardyce Nicoll, *World Drama from Aeschylus to Anouilh* (London: Harrap, 1976), pp. 125–31.

24. For background reading, see J. P. Wickersham Crawford, *Spanish Drama before Lope de Vega* (Philadelphia: University of Pennsylvania Press, 1967); also Melveena McKendrick, *Theatre in Spain*.

25. See Allardyce Nicoll, *World Drama*, pp. 147–53 and 83–8.

26. The subject is briefly discussed in Melveena McKendrick, *Theatre in Spain*, pp. 137–9. A good study of the subject in Spanish is Eugenio Asensio, *Itinerario del entremés desde Lope de Rueda a Quiñones de Benavente*, pp. 77–81.

27. Sometimes the second Interlude was replaced by a dance, (McKendrick, *Theatre in Spain*, p. 137).

28. According to the Prologue to a collection of Interludes by Quiñones de Benavente (*La Jocosería*, 1645), 'If an actor-manager took two Interludes by this witty writer and added them to a bad play, they served as crutches to keep it from falling; by adding them to a good play, they served as wings that carried it to even greater heights.'

29. Lope de Vega, in his *New Art of Writing Plays at this Time* (*Arte nuevo de hacer comedias en este tiempo*), defines Interludes as 'old-style comedies' ('comedias antiguas'), 'consisting of a single action, involving ordinary people' ('plebeya gente'); he adds, 'an Interlude with a king in it has never been seen'. A curious comment from a man who thought nothing of putting kings and ordinary people into his own full-length plays!

30. See Agustín de la Granja, *Entremeses y mojigangas de Calderón para sus autos sacramentales* (Granada: Universidad de Granada, 1981).

31. For example, Nicholas Spadaccini, 'Writing for Reading: Cervantes's Aesthetics of Reception in the *Entremeses.*' See also Miguel de Cervantes, *El rufián dichoso: Pedro de Urdemalas*, ed. Jenaro Talens y Nicholas Spadaccini (Madrid: Cátedra, 1986), pp. 22–34. The same authors further develop this thesis in *Through the Shattering Glass: Cervantes and the Self-Made World.* (See also my section 'Cervantes and his Critics'.)

32. The *Prologue* suggests that his desire to avenge himself on the curmudgeonly actor-manager and to free himself from the frustrations of the theatre world was another strong influence in his decision.

33. See Melveena McKendrick, *Theatre in Spain*, pp. 261–6. J. M. Ruano de la Haza compares two versions of *La vida es sueño*, one intended for performance, the other for readers, in *La primera versión de 'La vida es sueño' de Calderón* (Liverpool: Liverpool University Press, 1992).

34. An account of the history and popularity of Golden-Age plays in print in this period is given by Edward M. Wilson and Don W. Cruickshank, *Samuel Pepys's Spanish Plays* (London: The Bibliographical Society, 1980), pp. 85–120.

35. See, for example, Jill Syverson-Stork, *Theatrical Aspects of the Novel: A Study of 'Don Quijote'* (Valencia: Albatros, 1986). Cory Reed points to the lack of evidence that the published version of *Eight Plays and Eight Interludes* was successful with readers, noting that a new edition did not appear until 1749 (*The Novelist as Playwright, p. 2*).

36. Cory A. Reed addresses this question very effectively (*The Novelist as Playwright*, pp. 5–36). Among critics who believe that Cervantes wrote all his plays primarily to be performed on stage, see John J. Allen, 'Some Aspects of the Staging of Cervantes' Plays', *Crítica Hispánica*, II (1989), pp. 7–16. See also my section 'Cervantes and his Critics'.

37. *The Novelist as Playwright*, pp. 183–5.

38. Nicholas Spadaccini, 'Writing for Reading', pp. 167–72. Spadaccini shows how, in *The Marvellous Puppet Show*, Cervantes ridicules the notion of peasant honour and purity of blood as exemplified by Lope's popular play *Peribáñez y el Comendador de Ocaña* (*Peribáñez and the Commander of Ocaña*).

39. The last lines of the play underscore this point:

> OCAÑA: Some because they have no wish to,
> Some because they can't achieve it:
> In the end no one gets married.
> I beg you'll listen to my tale
> And never doubt the truth of it:
> This Entertaining Comedy
> Does not conclude with wedding bells!

Another play in the collection, *Pedro de Urdemalas*, also draws attention to the lack of 'wedding bells' at its conclusion.

40. His 1977 study of Cervantes's theatre is titled *Cervantès, dramaturge: Un théâtre à naître* (*Cervantes as Playwright: A Theatre Before its Time*).

NOTE ON THE TRANSLATION

In making this translation, I have primarily relied upon the text of the *Entremeses* edited by Nicholas Spadaccini (1982). Wherever a doubt has arisen about the accuracy of the text (e.g. a typographical error or a problematic transcription) I have consulted the facsimile edition of the plays (published by the Real Academia Española in 1984). Other editions of the *Entremeses* which I have consulted (in particular for the purpose of interpreting some obscure references) are listed at the beginning of my 'Notes to the Text'. Translations of Spanish texts are my own, except where otherwise identified. In the case of *Don Quixote*, quotations are from the English edition translated by J. M. Cohen. As a general rule I have omitted accents in Spanish names, except where they may be of assistance to the English-speaking reader, for example, Escarramán. I have also added cast lists.

Cervantes's *Entremeses* present a special challenge to the translator, not only because the understanding of a humorous text depends so much on an understanding of the culture behind it, but also because Cervantes's humour derives primarily from a brilliant play on language. The translator is faced with the challenge of evoking a similar range of responses in the modern reader/spectator through a series of carefully selected equivalents. In recreating the *Entremeses* in an English version I have attempted to convey all the nuances of the original while, at the same time, leaving the text open to the reader's interpretation wherever the meaning seems deliberately ambiguous. I also hope that my version will make readers aware that these pieces are not just intended to be read, but also to be performed. With this in mind, I have attempted to produce a text that can be staged today without compromising the integrity of the original.

Cervantes often gives witty names to his characters as a way of telling us what to expect from them. Translating those names can be a frustrating exercise. For example, in *The Marvellous Puppet Show* the word play involved cannot be adequately communicated in modern English. On the other hand, the names of the characters in *The Election of the Magistrates of Daganzo* are more readily translatable as Hoof, Sneeze, Crusty, Clod, etc., creating much the same comic effect in English as they do in Spanish.

I have given special attention to the rhythm of speech patterns, believing this to be one of the keys to successful translation. Since speech patterns in English and Spanish are very different, it is important not to force them into similar moulds – a practice that often leads to a stilted translation. Instead, I have looked to models like Bertolt Brecht, whose habit of interpolating verse and song in prose dialogue offers an interesting way of dealing with obscure passages (see, for example, the beginning of *Sir Vigilant*). For this reason I sometimes use rhyming couplets where they do not exist in the original, believing that they manage to convey the spirit, if not the letter, of what Cervantes intended. In the case of the two Interludes that he wrote in verse, I have opted for a loose iambic pentameter because it comes closest to English speech patterns. At the same time the restrictions imposed by this metrical straitjacket point up the playful irony conveyed by Cervantes's own choice of verse that at times verges on doggerel.

A Note on Seventeenth-century Currency

The currency of Cervantes's day included the 'maravedí' (the smallest unit), the silver 'real' and the gold 'escudo' (which took the place of the 'ducat', the gold coinage issued by the Catholic Kings). I have used 'ducats' rather than 'escudos' in *The Man who Pretended to be from Biscay* because the word is more familiar to an English-speaking reader. Jean Canavaggio estimates both coins to have been worth about $30 (£15) according to today's values, while Melveena McKendrick puts their 'psychological value' during Cervantes's lifetime at only $10 (£5). When Doña Guiomar (in *The Divorce Court Judge*) claims that her husband comes home empty-handed 'sin que le hayan dado un real de barato', I translate this as 'without a shilling to show for his pains' (the 'real' seems to have been the equivalent of an English pound or an American dollar today). The braggart soldier in *Sir Vigilant* gives the boy begging alms eight 'maravedíes' ('un cuarto de a ocho') if he will stay away from Cristina's house for four days. In my version he offers him eight farthings – in other words, a ridiculously small sum of money.

EIGHT INTERLUDES

To the Reader[1]

Dear Reader, I can do no less than beg your forgiveness if in this Prologue I should stray somewhat from my accustomed modesty. A few days ago while some friends and I were discussing plays and such matters, we proposed some ways of improving and refining them that, in my view, brought them close to perfection. The question came up of who in Spain first lifted them out of the cradle, gave them importance and turned them into a spectacle. As the oldest person present, I said that I recalled seeing Lope de Rueda perform and that he was outstanding both in his acting and his intelligence.[2] He was a native of Seville, a metal-beater by trade – that is to say he made gold leaf. He wrote such admirable pastoral poetry that no one at that time or since has written better. Even though I was just a boy then and not a practised judge of the quality of his poetry, yet I can still remember some of it and, with the wisdom of my maturer years, I find my first impression to have been correct. If the subject did not fall outside the scope of this Prologue, I would quote some of his poetry here to prove my point.

When that famous Spaniard was alive, an actor-manager's equipment could be packed into a single bag; it consisted more or less of four white goatskin jackets embossed with gilt, along with the same number of false beards, wigs and shepherd's crooks. The plays were in the form of conversations, rather like eclogues, between two or three shepherds and the odd shepherdess. They were enlivened and supplemented by several Interludes, usually involving a black woman, a pimp, a fool, or sometimes a Biscayan.[3] This Lope could play any of these characters, as well as many others, with the greatest skill and in the most lifelike way imaginable.

In those days there were no stage machines, nor skirmishes between Moors and Christians, either on foot or on horseback. No figure appeared, or seemed to appear, from the bowels of the earth through the space beneath the stage, for the stage consisted of four benches arranged in a square with four to six planks laid on top, at a height of some four handspans. There were certainly no cloud machines descending with angels or human souls. The stage was bare except for an old blanket that was pulled from one side to the other on two pieces of rope so as to form what they call the tiring room. Behind this sat the musicians, who used to sing some old ballad with no accompaniment – not even a guitar.

Lope de Rueda was so famous and highly regarded that when he died in Córdoba, they buried him there in the church between the choir-stalls, next to the tomb of that well-known madman, Luis López.

After Lope de Rueda came Navarro, a native of Toledo, who was famous for his portrayal of a cowardly pimp.[4] He somewhat improved the stage decoration, gave up carrying the costumes in a sack and put them in chests and trunks instead. He brought the musicians onto the stage, whereas previously they had done their singing behind the blanket. He broke with the custom of having all the actors perform with false beards and made them do without those defences, unless they were playing the part of old men or other characters who needed to disguise their faces. He invented stage machinery, cloud machines, thunder and lightning effects, and battles on stage. However, none of this reached the lofty pinnacle which it occupies at present.

Here is a fact that no one can deny, although it requires me to go beyond the limits of modesty: *Life in Algiers*, which I wrote, was performed in the theatres in Madrid; also *The Siege of Numantia* and *The Naval Battle*.[5] I was bold enough to reduce these plays to three acts, instead of the customary five. I was the first to portray on stage the imaginings and secret thoughts of the soul by bringing allegorical figures into the theatre, to the general pleasure and applause of the public. At that time I wrote some twenty or thirty plays, which were performed without causing cucumbers, or any other missiles, to be thrown at them.[6] They were all received without provoking whistles, catcalls or other such uproar. Then, with other things to occupy my time, I put aside my pen and wrote no more plays. Along came the great Lope de Vega, one of nature's prodigies, and made off with the theatrical crown. The actors all became his slaves and were subject to his rule. He filled the world with his own pleasing and well-made plays – so many, in fact, that they already exceed ten thousand pages.[7] What is more, he has seen them all brought to the stage, or at least been told of their performance. And if some people (and there are many) have dared to emulate his success, even when counted together they have failed to write one half of what he alone has produced.

Nevertheless, since no one is favoured with all of God's gifts, we must also pay tribute to Dr Ramón, who was second to Lope in the number of plays he wrote. Let us also give credit to Bachelor Miguel Sánchez for his highly ingenious plots; Dr Mira de Amescua, the pride of our nation, for his dignity; Canon Tárraga for his good sense and many sound ideas; Guillén de Castro for his sweet lyricism; and Aguilar for his wit. Nor should we forget the lavish spectacle of plays by Luis Vélez de Guevara, the plays that are emerging from the lively wit of Don Antonio de Galarza and the promising talent of Gaspar de Avila, as seen in *The Deceits of Love*. All these and others have helped to build the empire of the mighty Lope.[8]

A few years ago I returned to my former leisurely way of life and, believing that I could still rely on my old reputation, I started to write some new plays. But the birds of yesteryear had flown the nest. I mean to say that no actor-manager wanted them, although it was common knowledge that they were available. So I put them away in a chest and condemned them to eternal silence.

At that time a bookseller said that he would have bought them if a licensed actor-manager[9] had not told him that, although much could be expected of my prose, my poetry was worthless. I must confess that this caused me much grief and I said to myself: 'Either I'm not the man I once was, or times have changed for the better – which is contrary to common belief, since we always praise what is past.' I looked over my plays again, along with some Interludes that I had put away as well, and found them good enough to show to other actor-managers less scrupulous and more discerning than their dim-witted colleagues. I took the risk and sold them to the aforementioned bookseller, who published them exactly as you find them here.[10] He paid me a reasonable sum and I took the money gladly, and paid no further heed to bickering actors.

I would like them to be the best in the world – or, at least, reasonably good. You shall judge for yourself, dear Reader. If you find something good in them, tell my slanderous manager that he should change his opinion, for my words offend no one. Let him take note that they are not full of arrant nonsense and that the poetry is what is required in plays: that is to say, in keeping with the least exalted of the three accepted styles. What is more, the language employed in the Interludes is appropriate to the characters who appear in them. By way of compensation, I am offering him a play that I am writing called *Deceptive Appearances*[11] and, if I am not mistaken, it will be to his liking. With that, God give you good health and grant me forbearance.

THE DIVORCE COURT
JUDGE

INTRODUCTION

According to the Catholic religion, marriage is a sacrament that can only be broken by death, or by other causes that are worse than death itself; these may excuse a married couple from living together without, however, undoing the knot that bound them together.

(Miguel de Cervantes, *The Trials of Persiles and Sigismunda*)

While the Catholic Church maintained that the sacrament of marriage was indissoluble, it nevertheless permitted couples to seek a legal separation on certain grounds such as incompetence on the part of one of the partners. Such a separation, termed a divorce 'a mensa et thoro', was not considered to be a dissolution of the marriage. Petitions for separation were heard by an ecclesiastical court, presided over by a judge acting according to canon law.

The action of the Interlude involves the appearance in court of three couples and a man, ending with an adjournment for lack of evidence and a song and dance advocating reconciliation or, perhaps, resigned acceptance of the *status quo*. Critics are divided in their views of this Interlude: some interpret it as an affirmation of Cervantes's belief in the sanctity of Christian marriage, while others take the opposite view; some find evidence in it of his anti-feminism, others see it as an autobiographical piece. A recent study suggests that it should be read as a comment on the bureaucratic and legalistic attitude to marriage in seventeenth-century Spain, as well as a reaction to the new economic reality that turned women into 'objects of exchange'.[12]

What is to be made of such a wide choice of interpretations? Certainly the Interlude appears to offer a cynical view of marriage, but it is also one that is in keeping with the traditional treatment of the subject in other examples of low comedy, from Aristophanes and Plautus to medieval farce, ballad literature ('romances'), or the books of popular proverbs ('refraneros'). As comic motif the battle of the sexes is ageless and infinitely variable. In *The Divorce Court Judge* Cervantes is even-handed in his depiction of the warring factions. If we sympathise with Mariana, who has to put up with her tiresome old man, we can also feel sorry for him, who asks for nothing better than to be free of his nagging wife. Much the same can be said for the two couples who follow them.

Although the porter's description of his absent wife makes her out to be a shrew, it is evident that he is largely responsible for his own unhappiness because he married a prostitute while he was in a drunken stupor. Indeed, the marriages of the other plaintiffs also involved some kind of deceit or false expectation: the old man contracted marriage with a young wife; Guiomar was misled by the soldier's well-dressed appearance into thinking that he would be able to support her in a style equal to her aspirations; Aldonza believed that her future husband was a qualified doctor.

The plaintiffs have at least one thing in common: the bargains they contracted have all turned sour, or become intolerable with the passage of time. The Judge dismisses this inescapable fact of life as insufficient grounds for divorce. 'I find no reason to unmarry you,' he tells Mariana. 'You enjoyed the fruit when it was ripe, now you must put up with the rotting remains.'

The song that the musicians sing at the end of the Interlude echoes the theme:

> Facing the problems fair and square
> Is one good way to clear the air;
> Haggle and shout when you sign the lease,
> The rest of the year you can live in peace.

and they conclude:

> It's better then to kiss and mend
> Than choose divorce and make an end.

Similarly, the celebrations that end the play are given by an estranged couple whom the Judge had 'recently brought to their senses, persuading them to kiss and make up'.

Is this simply a conventional 'happy-ever-after' ending, in keeping with what was expected of the genre? It may be noted that several of the *Exemplary Novels* also end in summary fashion, as if their author were more interested in the unfolding of the story than in its conclusion.

It is possible that the Interlude was one of the two added at the last moment and that, in his haste to prepare the volume for publication, Cervantes did not have time to finish revising it. As it stands it is a curiously unstructured piece. One critic has called it 'a chain of episodes without action, protagonist or proper resolution.[13] Those who believe that Cervantes revised his Interludes for a reading public cite this example in support of their argument.

On the other hand, Stanislav Zimic sees in this piece a typical example of Cervantine irony: there is no possibility of a satisfactory resolution of the problem, the characters are trapped forever in their domestic hell. Zimic argues that the open-endedness of the piece is deliberate, in accord with Cervantes's belief that the knowing reader ('el lector discreto') would be aware of the implicit irony. That readers have largely failed to appreciate the piece until our own time is a further indication of the depth and subtlety of Cervantes's art.[14]

It may be that in our search for neat categories and tidy answers we are asking too much of this text; that it can, in fact, accommodate to some extent most of the interpretations that have been put forward. We need to take into account its reliance on traditional sources, on certain events in Cervantes's own life and his observation of the life and events around him. No doubt it does reflect the spirit of his times, the contemporary attitude to women, to marriage and, especially, the prevailing mood of world-weariness ('desengaño').[15] At the same time, we should not forget that it is the nature of Interludes to send up serious topics – not to trivialise them, but rather to draw attention to their importance. This is the true function of comedy.

CAST

JUDGE
NOTARY
ATTORNEY
OLD MAN
MARIANA
SOLDIER
GUIOMAR
SURGEON
ALDONZA DE MINJACA
PORTER
TWO MUSICIANS

THE DIVORCE COURT JUDGE

(El juez de los divorcios)

The JUDGE *enters with the* NOTARY *and the* ATTORNEY.
He takes his seat. Enter an OLD MAN[16] *and his wife*, MARIANA.

MARIANA: At last the divorce judge has taken his place in court!
Enough of this shilly-shallying. This time I am going to be set
free – free as a bird![17]

OLD MAN: For pity's sake, Mariana, there's no need to bellow
from the roof-tops. Speak more softly. God's wounds, you're
deafening the neighbours with your shouting. The judge is
right there, so just lower your voice and tell him what's
wrong.

JUDGE: Well, good people, what's your quarrel?

MARIANA: Divorce, divorce, divorce. A thousand times divorce!

JUDGE: Who from, madam? On what grounds?

MARIANA: Who from? From this old crock here.

JUDGE: On what grounds?

MARIANA: I can't abide his peevish demands any longer. I refuse
to look after his countless ailments all the time. My parents
didn't bring me up to be a nurse and handmaid. A very good
dowry I brought this old bag of bones who's consuming my
life. When he first got his hands on me, my face was as bright
and polished as a mirror, and now it's as crumpled as a
widow's veil. Please, your honour, unmarry me or I'll hang
myself. Just look at the furrows I've got from the tears I shed
every day that I'm married to this walking skeleton.

JUDGE: Cry no more, madam. Cease your bawling and dry
your tears. I'll see that justice is done.

MARIANA: Let me cry, your honour. It's such a comfort. In
well-ordered societies a marriage should be reviewed every
three years, and dissolved or renewed like a rental agreement.[18] It shouldn't have to last a lifetime and bring everlast-
ing misery to both parties.

JUDGE: If that policy were practical, desirable, or financially profitable, it would already be law.[19] But, madam, you must be specific about your reasons for seeking a divorce.

MARIANA: For one thing, my husband is in the winter of life, while I'm in the spring of youth. For another, I lose my sleep getting up in the middle of the night to put hot cloths and poultices on his belly; then I have to fetch him one bandage after another – what I'd give to see him condemned to be bandaged to a post! I have to prop up his pillows at night and bring him cough syrup for the congestion in his lungs. What's more, I have to put up with the stench of his breath – it stinks to high heaven.

NOTARY: He must have a rotten tooth in there.

OLD MAN: That can't be. The devil knows I don't have a tooth in my head!

ATTORNEY: I believe there's a law that recognises bad breath as sufficient cause for a wife to leave her husband, or vice versa.

OLD MAN: The fact is, gentlemen, that the bad breath she complains about doesn't come from my rotten teeth (because I haven't any), or from my stomach (which is in excellent condition). It comes from her ill will. Gentlemen, you don't know what this woman is like. I swear that if you did you'd avoid her like the plague, or else treat her like the devil. She's rude, quarrelsome and capricious, and I've been an uncomplaining martyr for twenty-two years.[20] For the past two years she's been coaxing and pushing me towards the grave. She's almost deafened me and driven me half mad with her scolding and arguing. If she nurses me, as she claims, it's always with nagging, instead of with the gentle voice and manner that you expect from someone who ministers to the sick. I swear, gentlemen, that, thanks to her, I'm the one who's dying, while she's thriving off me – after all, she has complete control over my estate.

MARIANA: Your estate indeed! Everything you own was bought with my dowry! Like it or not, half the belongings we've acquired since we married are mine![21] If I die tomorrow I won't leave you a farthing – that's how much I love you!

JUDGE: Tell me, sir, when you married your wife, weren't you healthy, carefree and in fine fettle?

OLD MAN: I've told you that I've been married to her for twenty-two years – like a galley slave under the command of a Calabrian renegade.[22] When I met her I could satisfy all her demands.

MARIANA: That was a nine-day wonder!

JUDGE: Silence, woman. Hold your tongue for God's sake! I find no reason to unmarry you. You enjoyed the fruit when it was ripe, now you must put up with the rotting remains. A husband can't be expected to weather the passage of time. Time waits for no man. Forget the ills he causes you today and remember the pleasures he gave you when he was in his prime. I don't want to hear another word from you!

OLD MAN: Your honour, you'd do me a great favour if you'd put an end to my misery and release me from my prison. I'm at breaking point, so if you don't release me now you'll just be handing me back to my torturer. If that's not possible, let's agree on one thing: she can shut herself away in a convent and I'll go to a monastery. We'll divide the estate and live out the rest of our lives in peace and to the glory of God.

MARIANA: To hell with that! A fine idea to shut me away! A convent's for a girl who enjoys life behind bars, with everything passed through a turnstile and visits supervised by the nuns![23] Try shutting yourself away – it makes no difference to you: you can't see or hear; your feet will hardly carry you and your hands are useless. I'm in good health, in full possession of my senses. I'm not playing my cards close to my chest. I mean to lay them all on the table where they can be seen.

NOTARY: This woman doesn't mince her words!

ATTORNEY: The husband's a sensible man, but there's a limit to his patience.

JUDGE: Well, I can't grant you a divorce. I find no fault at all . . . [24]

Enter a well-groomed SOLDIER *with his wife*, GUIOMAR[25]

GUIOMAR: Thank Heaven for this opportunity to speak to your honour. I beseech you with all my heart, be pleased to release me from marriage to this creature.

JUDGE: What do you mean by 'this creature'? Doesn't he have a name? It would be better if you at least referred to him as 'this man'.

GUIOMAR: If he were a man I wouldn't be trying to end the marriage.

JUDGE: What is he, then?

GUIOMAR: A block of wood.

SOLDIER: (*aside*) My God, only a block of wood would take what I put up with and never say a word. Perhaps if I don't try to defend myself and let her have her say, the judge will find against me. He'll think he's punishing me, but he'll be setting me free, just as surely as if he released a prisoner from the dungeons of North Africa.

ATTORNEY: Watch your language, madam, and get to the point without insulting your husband. His honour the Judge, whom you see before you, will see that you are treated fairly.

GUIOMAR: Why, sirs, what's wrong with calling a statue a block of wood if it behaves like one?

MARIANA: It sounds as though this woman and I share a common complaint.

GUIOMAR: In short, sir, I'm saying that I was married off to this man (if that's what you insist on calling him), but this man isn't the one I married.

JUDGE: How's that? I don't follow you.

GUIOMAR: I mean that I thought I was marrying a man who was normal – you might say run-of-the-mill – but I soon found out he was a block of wood, just as I said. He can't tell his right hand from his left, and he makes no effort whatsoever to earn anything to support his family. He spends his morning at Mass or hanging around the Guadalajara Gate,[26] gossiping and exchanging lies and hearsay. In the afternoon, and sometimes in the morning too, he does the round of the gaming houses. There he joins the crowd of onlookers who hang around the gamblers in the hope of a tip – though they're heartily disliked by the people in charge.[27] He shows up for dinner around two o'clock without a shilling to show for his pains because they're no longer in a tipping mood. He goes out again, returns at midnight, has supper if he can find any leftovers, and if not, he blesses himself, gives a yawn and goes to bed. Then he can't sleep and tosses all night. I ask him what's wrong. He tells me he's composing a sonnet for a friend who wants an epitaph. He insists on being a poet, as if that weren't the worst-paid job in the world!

SOLDIER: My dear wife, everything you say is perfectly reasonable – just as everything I do is perfectly reasonable. If it were not so, I would have managed to get hold of some small official favour – like many clever wheedlers I know, who land themselves a staff of office and a small bad-tempered mule (the kind you can hire from a livery stable when they have nothing else available, and that comes without a groom). In one saddlebag they carry a clean shirt and collar, in the other a wedge of cheese, a loaf of bread and a wineskin; they're wearing their city clothes, with leggings and a single spur added for the journey; their commissions are gnawing at them inside their shirts.[28] Out across the Toledo Bridge[29] they clatter, urging on their stubborn mules; a few days later they send home a salted leg of pork and a length of unbleached linen – in short, items that can be bought cheap in the places they've been sent to, and that help to put food on the table at home. However, I enjoy neither job nor patronage. I don't know what to do because no one wants to hire a married man. With the gentry so tight-fisted and my wife so insistent, I've no choice, your honour, but to implore you to grant us a divorce.

GUIOMAR: There's something else, sir. Since I know my husband is so puny and inadequate, I do my best to help, but there's a limit: after all, I'm a respectable woman and I don't have to do anything I'd be ashamed of!

SOLDIER: On that score alone this woman deserves to be loved; but look beneath those scruples and you'll find the most ill-natured creature alive. She turns jealous for no reason at all, starts screaming without provocation, has far too high an opinion of herself and turns her nose up at me because I'm poor. But the worst part, your honour, is that in return for remaining faithful to me, she expects me to put up with her bad temper and disagreeable ways.

GUIOMAR: Well, why not? Seeing that I'm such a virtuous woman, why shouldn't you treat me with the honour and respect that I deserve?

SOLDIER: Just listen to me, wife – let these gentlemen hear what I have to say to you: why do you keep harping on how virtuous you are, when that's what any self-respecting Christian lady of decent family is expected to be? Just imagine women wanting their husbands to respect them for being faithful and modest! As if that were enough to make them perfect! They don't notice that all their other virtues have fallen through the cracks! What do I care that you're satisfied with your own moral standards? On the other hand, I care a great deal that you ignore your maid's immoral behaviour, that you're a spendthrift, and that you're constantly frowning, complaining and arguing; that you're angry, jealous, distracted, lazy, idle, and a lot more besides. That's enough to finish off two hundred husbands! Yet when all's said and done, your honour, my wife Mistress Guiomar doesn't have any of these vices and I admit that I'm a block of wood, good for nothing, negligent, a lazybones. So if for no other reason than to uphold the law, sir, you'll have to give us a separation. I make no objection to what my wife has said; I consider the case closed and I'll be glad to accept your judgment.

GUIOMAR: What objection could you possibly make? You provide nothing to eat, either for me or our servant (take note that I said servant, in the singular), and she's as skinny as a baby born before its time – doesn't eat enough to keep a cricket alive.

NOTARY: Order, there. Here come some more plaintiffs.

Enter a BARBER-SURGEON *dressed as a doctor,*[30]
with his wife, ALDONZA DE MINJACA

SURGEON: I come to you, your honour, to beg you to grant me a separation from my wife, Aldonza de Minjaca, on four principal counts.

JUDGE: You've made up your mind already. Tell me what the four counts are.

SURGEON: First, because I can no more put up with her than with all the devils in hell. Second, for reasons that she's aware of. Third, for reasons I can't mention. Fourth, to save my soul from the devil. Just see if I'm going to put up with her company for the rest of my life!

ATTORNEY: You've more than stated your case.

ALDONZA: Your honour, listen to me. I'll have you know that if my husband's asking for a divorce on four counts, then I'm asking for one on four hundred. First, because every time I set eyes on him I believe I'm seeing the devil himself. Second, because he decieved me when I married him: he told me he was a qualified doctor and then he turned out to be a mere surgeon – someone who bandages and attends to minor ailments – he's a far cry from a real doctor. Third, because he's jealous of everything, even the sun that shines on me. Fourth, since I can't abide him, I'd like to put a million miles between us.

NOTARY: How the devil can anyone ever make these two clocks chime together? They don't even keep the same time!

ALDONZA: Fifth . . .

JUDGE: Madam, madam, if you plan to give us every one of your four hundred reasons, I'm not disposed to hear them and, besides, there isn't time. We'll hold your case over pending further evidence – so you can go now, God rest you. We have other cases to consider.

SURGEON: What more evidence do you need, since I refuse to die in her company and she doesn't want to live in mine?

JUDGE: If that were sufficient reason for a divorce, there'd be no end of couples in a hurry to shake off the matrimonial yoke.

Enter a PORTER, *wearing his quartered hood.*[31]

PORTER: Mister Judge, sir, I'm a porter – I won't deny that – but I'm a Christian[32] through and through and a truly honest man. If I didn't sometimes get hold of the wine, or, rather, if the wine didn't get hold of me, I could have been a steward in the porters' brotherhood by now. I could say more, but to get to the point, I'd like to inform your honour that once, when I was very sick from my perilous encounters with Bacchus, I promised to marry a lady of the night. When I recovered I kept my word and saved the woman from sin by making her my wife. I set her up selling fruit and vegetables in the market, but she's grown so stuck up and bad-tempered that she gets into a fight with everyone who comes to her stall.[33] Sometimes it's because she gives short measure, or, nine times out of ten, because someone touches the fruit. When that happens she throws a lead weight at their heads, or wherever she happens to aim, and curses them down to the fourth generation. Her gossiping neighbours don't give her a moment's peace and my sword goes in and out like a switchblade in her defence.[34] We scarcely earn enough to pay the fines she gets for selling short and starting fights. If it please your honour, I'd like to be quit of her, or perhaps you could make her less of a shrew, more gentle and ladylike. If you'll do that, your honour, I'll see you get free delivery of all the charcoal you need this summer, for I've a good deal of influence with my fellow porters.[35]

SURGEON: I know this fellow's wife and she's just as bad as my Aldonza. Need I say more than that?

JUDGE: See here, good people, although some of you have made a good case for divorce, you must still present everything in writing with the support of witnesses. So I'm adjourning the court for the time being. But what have we here? People playing guitars in my court? This is something new, indeed!

Enter TWO MUSICIANS.

MUSICIAN: Your honour, do you remember that estranged couple you recently brought to their senses, persuading them to kiss and make up? Well, they're throwing a big party at their house and they've sent us to ask your honour to be good enough to join them.

JUDGE: I'll be delighted to do so. I trust all these people will find as peaceful an end to their troubles.

ATTORNEY: If that were to happen the notaries and attorneys of this court would all starve. No, no, let every couple seek a divorce. When all's said and done, most of them end up as they were and we stand to gain by their quarrels and foolishness.

MUSICIANS: Well, for now, let's go and join in the fun.

(*The* MUSICIANS *sing.*)
To every couple, man and wife,
There comes a time of open strife;
It's better then to kiss and mend
Than choose divorce and make an end.

Facing the problems fair and square
Is one good way to clear the air;
Haggle and shout when you sign the lease,
The rest of the year you can live in peace.[36]

That's the way to revive your pride,
And kindle the flame you thought had died.
It's better then to kiss and mend
Than choose divorce and make an end.

It's said that jealousy brings pain
That saps your strength and slows your brain,
But if the cause is fair as well,
The pain's divine and not pure hell.

I hereby cite an expert's view,
For Love himself swears this is true.
It's better then to kiss and mend
Than choose divorce and make an end.

THE WIDOWED PIMP

THE ELECTION OF THE MAGISTRATES OF
DAGANZO

These are the only Interludes that Cervantes wrote in verse, a fact that may indicate that they were late additions.[37] Apart from that, they represent two satirical views of quite different aspects of contemporary society, one urban, the other rural.

In setting *The Widowed Pimp* against the background of Madrid (along with the majority of his Interludes) Cervantes was evoking a city that he came to know well during the last years of his life. After 1606, when the Court became established permanently there, Madrid grew rapidly in both size and notoriety. In the words of a contemporary observer, it was 'the Spanish Babylon'.[38] Like Seville before it, Madrid drew people from all backgrounds and levels of society, hopeful of finding fame and fortune by whatever means.

Among other marginal occupations, prostitution flourished, as contemporary records and the journals of foreign travellers attest. Although the authorities attempted to control prostitution by licensing establishments and paying the women a salary, this did not save them from exploitation by pimps who lived off their earnings in return for so-called protection.

Stanislav Zimic suggests that *The Widowed Pimp* is an audacious parody of the famous Eclogues written by the great sixteenth-century Castillian poet Garcilaso de la Vega. The Eclogues describe an idyllic pastoral setting in which shepherds become enamoured of nymphs and lament the sad death of one of them. Cervantes's Interlude turns this Virgilian image upside-down, substituting prostitutes and pimps for nymphs and shepherds. He also uses the same metrical measure as Garcilaso, while replacing the traditional pastoral imagery with ribald and irreverent allusions.[39] For his audience/readers, familiar with the terms of the parody, its effect must have been both subversive and hilarious.

The subtext of the piece is further enriched by a network of other topical and literary references. Amongst these is the appearance of the figure Escarramán, originally created by Cervantes's contemporary Francisco de Quevedo and subsequently popularised in bawdy songs and dances.[40] Spadaccini and Talens suggest that Cervantes introduces this picaresque anti-hero, 'the king of ruffians', as a parody of the custom whereby the king presides over the marriages that end so many *Comedias*, symbolically restoring social order and harmony.

The Widowed Pimp mocks convention in other ways: while it begins on a solemn note with the pimp Trampagos mourning his lost concubine, he is soon consoled by the appearance of his friends and the opportunity to choose a replacement for the dead woman. As grief gives way to merriment, we are reminded that this is a mirror image of everyday life: a world turned upside-down. The pimp's extravagant eulogies of his lost Pericona dwell on the sordid nature of her trade, her struggle to disguise her age and, finally, the disgusting nature of the syphilis that killed her. As well, she is praised for her constancy in terms worthy of a Christian saint, when in fact her steadfastness was shown in the pursuit of her less than saintly profession! Moreover, it is clear that the pimp's devotion to Pericona depended on her ability to maintain him financially, rather than on any bond of affection ('I've lost my Potosí, my silver mine . . .' he laments). Her would-be successors attempt to woo him with competing offers: 'I'm free as air with lots of cash to spare,' says one; 'I'm flush as well and ready for investment,' counters another; 'I offer all I have and maybe more . . .' promises the third. In choosing one of them, Trampagos ensures that his parasitic life will continue; no wonder that he is ready to forget Pericona and celebrate! It falls to one of the other prostitutes to reflect on the hollowness of her colleague's victory:

> She's taking risks. Don't envy her so fast:
> As catches go, Trampagos is not perfect.
> Just yesterday he buried Pericona,
> Today she's quite forgotten.

Even today, while much of the humour cannot be shared, *The Widowed Pimp* still bubbles with malicious fun and invites an imaginative re-creation on stage.

Of the eight Interludes only two, *The Election of Magistrates in Daganzo* and *The Marvellous Puppet Show*, have settings that are specifically rural. Yet both are far from depicting the idyllic *Beatus Ille* associated with literary conceptions of rural life. On the contrary, they ridicule the collective self-importance and individual pretensions of those who constitute provincial governance. As well, they reveal the prejudices and small-mindedness that typically characterise small communities. No doubt Cervantes was familiar with such places from his long years of travel and had encountered similar attitudes at first hand.

The Election of the Magistrates of Daganzo falls into two parts: the first, like *The Divorce Court Judge* and, to some extent, *The Widowed Pimp*, consists of an extended dialogue between groups of characters, with little indication of physical action. The second part introduces new characters – in this case a band of gypsy-musicians and a disapproving sexton – who provide diversion with song and dance and the tossing of the sexton in a blanket.

The subject of the Interlude appears to derive from an actual historical event well known in the time of Cervantes: the case of the feudal lord of Daganzo who refused to approve the appointment of magistrates elected by the town, on grounds that they were incompetent to serve.[41] With this incident as pretext, Cervantes creates his own scenario in which the town officials interview the four candidates for office. The fact that only one of these is chosen attests to the woeful inadequacy of the other candidates. Since the selection must still be approved by the feudal overlord in Toledo, it is clear, moreover, that the officials have very little authority in their own town.

The Interlude opens with the four officials preparing to interview the four candidates. Some critics consider this first section discursive and irrelevant; nevertheless, it serves to reveal the character of the officials as they posture and wrangle amongst themselves. Their names alone are indication of what we can expect of them: Bachelor Hoof (El Bachiller Pesuña) is pompous and self-important, given to quoting in Latin and correcting his companions;[42] Crusty (Panduro) and Alonso Stringbean (Algarroba), the two aldermen, are obviously old adversaries and do not miss an opportunity to score off each other; Peter Sneeze, the notary, tries to play a conciliatory role, but later in the piece he, too, is drawn into the game of trading racial slurs.

When the four labourers enter for examination we also know what to expect: Johnny Clod (Juan Berrocal) is a connoisseur of wines; Knuckleknees (Miguel Jarrete) is adept at killing birds with a catapult; Francis Puff (Francisco Humillos) is a skilled shoemaker and Peter Frog (Pedro Rana) has a remarkable memory. What we learn from their presence shows the limitations of their accomplishments: for the most part they are illiterate, boorish and narrow-minded. Only Peter Frog seems to be a worthy candidate when he promises to practise moderation and courtesy if he is made a judge (although his pledges are greeted with scepticism by Francis Puff).

This is more than a satire of provincial life; it also has a deeper irony that derives from the exposure of racial prejudice. All the characters – examiners and candidates alike – are anxious to prove that they belong to pure Christian stock, unsullied by any stain of alien blood.[43] In the play, as in society at large, this obsession focused primarily on the issue of Jewish blood.

A century after the expulsion of the Jews from the Peninsula, feelings of hostility and suspicion still persisted towards those who had remained as converts or 'New Christians'. They were perceived as a threat because of their successful participation in the professional and commercial life of the country. Although many Jewish converts embraced Christianity, changed their names and married into Christian families, they were treated with unrelenting fear and paranoia.[44]

This prejudice is the key to a number of references in *The Election of the Magistrates of Daganzo*. It explains Stringbean's assurance at the beginning of the play that his blood 'is purest Christian through and through'; as well as Puff's pride in being illiterate (because educated people were often Jewish 'Conversos'). It also puts Peter Frog in a different light: when Alderman Stringbean praises him for his memory, he cites as an example Frog's ability to recall some anti-Jewish verses; whereupon Crusty and the Notary immediately say they will vote for him, even before he appears for an interview. It may also be significant that at the end Crusty recalls that 'No one sings as well as our own Frog.' And Knuckleknees concurs:

> It isn't just his pleasant voice
> That makes him seem the obvious choice.

Peter Frog also holds stereotypical views about gypsies. Upon learning that a group of them have arrived and wish to perform, he warns,

> We must take good care
> Or else they'll rob us blind.

Nevertheless, the gypsy musicians take their revenge by mocking their hosts with absurd ditties praising them for being:

> Samsons of knowledge, learning and wit,
> And Solomons of muscle and grit.

How should we interpret the final episode, when a curmudgeonly sexton interrupts the festivities and reproaches them all for not taking their duties more seriously? Before punishing him with a traditional tossing in a blanket, Frog lectures him for presuming to tell others how to perform their duties:

> Leave governing to others better trained
> For what they have to do than all of us.
> If they are bad, then pray for their improvement;
> And if they're good, then pray they'll be long with us!

This is a surely a further piece of irony reflecting on the general inadequacy of those placed in authority. Nevertheless, some critics have seen it as a serious comment, citing as well Frog's earlier statement about the characteristics desirable in a magistrate.[45] These critics would have us believe that in these passages Cervantes is speaking to us in his own voice. It is unwise to assume any such thing, for Cervantes often seems to delight in putting apparently serious comments into the mouths of unlikely characters. In the inherently subversive world of the Interlude he places the burden of interpretation on readers and spectators, inviting them to complete the 'meaning' of the play in accordance with whatever context may seem appropriate to them.

CAST

THE WIDOWED PIMP

TRAMPAGOS
VADEMECUM
CHIQUIZNAQUE
REPULIDA
PIZPITA
MOSTRENCA
JUAN CLAROS
A MAN
TWO MUSICIANS
ESCARRAMÁN

THE WIDOWED PIMP

(El rufián viudo llamado Trampagos)

Enter the pimp TRAMPAGOS *in mourning clothes,*[46] *followed by his servant* VADEMECUM, *carrying a pair of fencing foils.*

TRAMPAGOS: Vademecum?[47]
VADEMECUM: Sir?
TRAMPAGOS:
Have you brought the foils?[48]
VADEMECUM: I have them here.
TRAMPAGOS: That's good. On guard!
Advance!
He makes suitable fencing gestures.
Now go and bring me out the high-backed chair,
And all the other chairs around the house.
VADEMECUM: What chairs? Did you say chairs? You'll be in
luck!
TRAMPAGOS: You oaf! Bring me the gauntlet and the buckler,
Also the bedstead.[49]
VADEMECUM: It's no use at all.
It's lost a leg.
TRAMPAGOS: Does that matter?
VADEMECUM: Certainly.
[*Exit* VADEMECUM]
TRAMPAGOS: Ah Pericona, my own Pericona –
Of course, the Council's Pericona too.
Your hour has come and I'm left quite alone.
What's worse, I dare not wonder where you've gone.
Such an exemplary life must surely mean
You've earned your place in hea . . . yet I'm still unable
To think of you up there among the angels.
Now life for me without you seems like death.
I should have stood beside you when you died,
For then I might have caught your fluttering soul,
Swallowed it and kept it in my belly.[50]

A wretched fate is ours! Who dares to trust it?
Or, as a famous poet might have said:
    My Pericona lived but yesterday.
    Today she's just a clod of frigid clay.
      Enter CHIQUIZNAQUE, *another pimp.*
CHIQUIZNAQUE: What's this, Trampagos? Can it really be
You've come to hate and loathe yourself so much,
Shrouding yourself in gloomy funeral weeds,
Clouding the sunshine in our den of thieves?
My dear Trampagos, you've gone far enough,
Your weeping and your sighing should now cease.
Instead of floods of tears and lamentations,
Give alms, say prayers and honour Pericona
With Masses for her soul – God give her peace –
They'll be of more avail than all your grieving.
TRAMPAGOS: Well, Mr Chiquiznaque, you certainly can spout
Like a theologian. Whilst I get used
To my new state, why don't we practise fencing?
Just grab a foil and try a lunge or two.
CHIQUIZNAQUE: Mr Trampagos, sir,
This is no time for fencing! It's a day
For condoling, sympathising and consoling.
And you suggest we try a lunge or two!
      Enter VADEMECUM *with an old, broken chair.*
VADEMECUM: Upon my soul, do not deny my master
A chance to thrust and parry with his foil,
For then you rob him of his very life.
TRAMPAGOS: Go in and find the gauntlet and the bench,
And don't forget the buckler, Vademecum.
VADEMECUM: I'll whip the roast pan, spit, and platters too!
      [VADEMECUM *goes out again.*]
TRAMPAGOS: Later on we'll practise my new riposte;
In my opinion it's unique and rare.
But now the thought of my dear angel's death
Has bound my hands and senses up with grief.
CHIQUIZNAQUE: How old was the poor lady when she died?
TRAMPAGOS: As far as all her friends and neighbours knew,
She was but thirty-two.
CHIQUIZNAQUE: A lusty age!
TRAMPAGOS: But if the truth be told, her actual age
Was fifty-six; yet she amazed me quite,

Such was her skill at hiding all the signs.
Such dyeing of grey hair, such girlish curls,
Transmuting silver into burnished gold!
Fifteen years have come and gone again
Since first she paid me dues. In that time,
I never had to fight on her behalf,
Nor bend my back to bear the cruel lash.[51]
While she was mine, my late lamented jewel,
Fifteen times the Lenten season came,
Deafening her with countless pious sermons,[52]
Throughout them all she kept her faith in me,
Unflinching, like the steadfast rock that stands
Against the pounding of the restless sea.
As she emerged from those relentless trials,
Those endless pleadings, prayers and supplications,
Which left her drenched with sweat and quite exhausted,
She'd say to me, 'I pray to Heaven, Trampagos,
My sufferings here for you will all be noted
And credited in payment for my sins.'

CHIQUIZNAQUE: Ah, what a triumph!
Rare example of undying constancy!
She's made herself immortal.

TRAMPAGOS: Beyond a doubt!
Through all those solemn moral exhortations
She shed no tears, her eyes were dry as straw:
You'd swear her soul was fashioned out of flint.

CHIQUIZNAQUE: A woman equal of those worthy matrons
In Greece and Rome who won the praise of all!
What caused her death?

TRAMPAGOS: What caused it? Almost nothing.
The doctors said she suffered with her liver,
And ailments in the hypochondriac region.[53]
With tamarisk infusions, they maintained,
She'd reach the ripe old age of seventy.

CHIQUIZNAQUE: She never took them?

TRAMPAGOS: No, she died.

CHIQUIZNAQUE: The fool!
She might have lived if she had kept on drinking
Until the Judgement Day! They didn't make
Her sweat enough.

TRAMPAGOS: Eleven times she sweated.[54]

(*Enter* VADEMECUM *with the aforementioned chairs.*)

CHIQUIZNAQUE: Did any help?

TRAMPAGOS: Well, almost every one.
  They left her feeling lively as a sapling,
  As ruddy as an apple or wild pear.

CHIQUIZNAQUE: It's said that suppurating ulcers sprang
  Out of her arms and legs.

TRAMPAGOS: Unhappy wretch,
  They spouted like Aranjuez;[55] none the less,
  Today our Mother Earth is feasting on
  The finest, whitest flesh that ever lay
  Enfolded in her deep maternal belly.
  Two years ago her breath began to sour;
  Until that time each fond embrace was like
  A whiff of wild carnations or sweet basil.

CHIQUIZNAQUE: It must have been a case of rotting gums,
  Or flux, that spoiled those pearls behind her smile:
  I mean, of course, her teeth and molars too.

TRAMPAGOS: One fine morning she arose without them.

CHIQUIZNAQUE: That's true enough, though I can tell you
                                            why:
  She went to bed without them, for her real teeth
  Numbered only five, you see. Twelve false ones
  Were hidden in the cavern of her mouth.

TRAMPAGOS: Who asked for your opinion, nincompoop?

CHIQUIZNAQUE: I repeat what's widely known.

TRAMPAGOS: Chiquiznaque
  Now I am able to recall quite well
  The riposte I spoke of; here, draw your foil,
  Assume the first position.

VADEMECUM: Stay a while:
  Keep the riposte suspended at that point.
  Here come the flies aswarming right on cue:
  The ladies Repulida and Pizpita,
  Madame Mostrenca and the doughty Juan.[56]

TRAMPAGOS: How welcome they are. They are truly welcome.

        Enter REPULIDA, PIZPITA, MOSTRENCA,
        and the pimp JUAN CLAROS.

TRAMPAGOS: A thousand greetings, friends.

JUAN: And also to you,

Good Señor Trampagos.

REPULIDA: May Heaven be pleased
To change your darkness into purest light!

PIZPITA: I pray that soon my eyes will see you peeling
Off that sad black garb you're wearing now.

MOSTRENCA: Jesus, what ghost of night do we have here?
Out of my sight, I say!

VADEMECUM: How very tactful!

TRAMPAGOS: I'd seem a monster or a cannibal,
A troglodyte, a boorish backbiter,
A schemer, savage, or a man-eater
If I should dress in any other way
At such a tragic time.

JUAN: He's right, you know.

TRAMPAGOS: I've lost my Potosí, my silver mine,[57]
The wall that propped the burden of my faults,
The tree that sheltered me from care and woe!

JUAN: Pericona was a pot of gold.

TRAMPAGOS: We'd open every night; by closing time
We had sixty copper pieces: no mean sum!
Now all of that lies rotting in the grave.

REPULIDA: I must confess to one small sin of envy
Of Pericona's wondrous diligence.
I do my best, as much as I can do,
I wish I could do more.

PIZPITA: Well, don't fret, dear.
It's better to know that God's on your side,
Than get up too early, I'm sure you'll agree.

VADEMECUM: That proverb fits the case just like a glove:
One day you'll sleep for ever, you poor fools!

MOSTRENCA: We're human too. There's hope for all of us
In God's wide world. I may not come to much,
Yet eat quite well and also keep my master
In handsome style and quite a lavish wardrobe.
A woman who has spirit is not ugly:
Only the devil's ugly.

VADEMECUM: She is right,
And what she says would carry added weight
If she should claim to be a pure young girl –
As well she may in every form and shape.

CHIQUIZNAQUE: Trampagos's shape is what fills me with pity.

TRAMPAGOS: I put this cloak on, while my brimming eyes
  Became twin vessels for distilling tears.
VADEMECUM: Of brandy?
TRAMPAGOS: Do I drink so much, you bastard?
VADEMECUM: Four washerwomen by the Segovia Bridge,[58]
  Rinsing their linen till it comes out clean,
  Are not able to match what you dispatch.
  I have no doubt your tears are straight firewater.
[CHIQUIZNAQUE]:[59] It's my belief the great and good
                                                Trampagos
  Should put a stop to his incessant weeping.
  'As it was in the beginning shall be now,'
  Is what I say to all his vanished joys.
  Shed those gloomy weeds, find a brand-new skirt:
  Let the living look to their daily bread;
  Leave the peace of the graveyard to the dead.
REPULIDA: That Chiquiznaque's quite the fount of wisdom.[60]
PIZPITA: I may be small, Trampagos, but my willingness
  To serve you is beyond all measure;
  I'm free as air with lots of cash to spare.
REPULIDA: I'm flush as well and ready for investment.
MOSTRENCA: I offer all I have and maybe more,
  And I'm no slouch.
REPULIDA: Dear Jesus! What's going on?
  Pizpita and Mostrenca ranged against me?
  You challenge me to fight in mortal combat,
  A jack-in-the-box[61] and a stupid dupe?
PIZPITA: By my sainted grandmother's sacred bones,
  Madam Dullwit and Lady Worse-than-Useless,[62]
  I wouldn't give a crooked farthing for you.
  Take a look at that stuck-up holier-than-thou,
  She wants to crow it over all of us!
MOSTRENCA: Not over me she won't, that's very certain.
  No one gets on my back without permission.
JUAN: Take note, you two, that I defend Pizpita.
CHIQUIZNAQUE: Then be advised that Repulida here
  Is sheltered by the wings of my protection.
VADEMECUM: That's done it! Now they'll tear each other
                                                apart.
  Out come the butcher knives. Just as I said,
  That's well and truly done it!

REPULIDA: Chiquiznaque,
  I've no need of someone to defend me.
  Just go away and I'll avenge myself.
  I'll use my own God-fearing hands to tear
  Her face, stained yellow like a quince with fever.
JUAN: Repulida, show respect for who I am!
PIZPITA: And I say, let her come. I dare her to.
  Just let that dough-faced woman come near me!
                    A MAN *enters in alarm.*
MAN: Juan Claros, fly, the constable's on his way.
  He's just down the street.
                              [*He exits in haste.*]
JUAN: By my father's corpse,
  I'm clearing off right now.
TRAMPAGOS: Just wait a moment:
  Don't be alarmed, my friends. I know the man,
  He's my pal – you have no need to fear him.
                    The other man returns.
MAN: He'll not come here, he went the other way.
                                          [*Exits*]
CHIQUIZNAQUE: My heart was in my mouth, I don't mind
                                          saying,
  For I've been banished.[63]
TRAMPAGOS: Even if he came
  He wouldn't harm you, and I know full well
  He wouldn't squeal because his palm is greased.
VADEMECUM: Call off your quarrel. Permit my master
  To choose the match that fits his needs the best,
  Or, should I say, that strikes his fancy most!
REPULIDA: I agree.
PIZPITA: And so do I.
MOSTRENCA: And I.
VADEMECUM: Thank Heaven!
  I've found a quick solution to this problem!
TRAMPAGOS: I'll risk my neck and choose.
MOSTRENCA: God guide your
                                          choice.
REPULIDA: If you risk your neck, Trampagos, your choice
  Will also be at risk.
TRAMPAGOS: I was misguided.
  I'll make my choice a safe one.

MOSTRENCA: May God guide you.

TRAMPAGOS: I here declare my choice is Repulida.

JUAN: (*to* CHIQUIZNAQUE) We each must lie in the bed that
                                          we have made.

CHIQUIZNAQUE: Bed or no bed, she's a rather tasty dish.

REPULIDA: I'm yours. So place the mark of your true slave[64]
  On either cheek. (*They kiss.*)

PIZPITA: O you little sorceress!

MOSTRENCA: She's taking risks. Don't envy her so fast:
  As catches go, Trampagos is not perfect:
  Just yesterday he buried Pericona,
  Today she's quite forgotten.

REPULIDA: That's well said.

TRAMPAGOS: Vademecum, bundle up this cloak,
  Ask our leader[65] to loan me a dozen shillings
  As a special favour.

VADEMECUM: I think I can do better
  And lend you fourteen.

TRAMPAGOS: Be off, then, waste no time
  And bring twelve litres of the finest wine.
  Put wings upon your feet.

VADEMECUM: And on my shoulders.
           [*Exit* VADEMECUM *with the cloak.* TRAMPAGOS *is left
                              in a state of undress.*]

TRAMPAGOS: God's blood, if I had worn that cloak much
                                                  longer
  They might have laid me in my grave tomorrow!

REPULIDA: Light of my eyes, which now are your eyes too,
  You look a great deal better in that costume
  Than in that drab and melancholy outfit!
           Enter TWO MUSICIANS, *without their guitars.*

FIRST MUSICIAN: Hot on the scent of that wine jug we come,
  My partner and I.

TRAMPAGOS: It's good to see you here.
  Where are your guitars?

FIRST MUSICIAN: We left them at my house.
  Vademecum can fetch them.

SECOND MUSICIAN: So he can,
  But I'll go instead.

FIRST MUSICIAN: And while you're about it,
  Tell my good wife that if a client comes

Who wants a shave, he'll have to wait a while.[66]
I'm only going to take a swig or six,
Then sing a song or two and get me home.
I can see that Mister Trampagos here
Is in the mood for merriment again.

            [SECOND MUSICIAN *exits*. VADEMECUM *returns*.]

VADEMECUM: The wineskin's just outside.

TRAMPAGOS: Bring it to me.

VADEMECUM: There are no cups.

TRAMPAGOS: We have no need for them
We've not yet christened our new chamber pot.[67]
So bring it here. A curse upon your head,
You'd even bring dishonour to a duke.

VADEMECUM: Don't be alarmed, we'll give you all a brimful,
And more than one, if you'll take off your hats.
(*aside*) Upon my soul! This must be a deserter.

      A man enters, dressed like a prisoner,
      with a chain hanging from his shoulder.
      He stares intently at everyone and they at him.

REPULIDA: Jesus! Is this a dream? What have we here?
Escarramán himself? No doubt whatever!
Escarramán, my love, come to my arms,
The inspiration of our band of thieves!

TRAMPAGOS: Escarramán, Escarramán, my friend,
How can this be? Have you been turned to stone?
Break your silence, speak to us, your friends!

PIZPITA: What clothes are those? What means that heavy
                           chain?
Are you by chance a ghost? Here, let me touch you . . .
No, you are flesh and blood.

MOSTRENCA: You're right, old girl,
It's really him, although he holds his tongue.

ESCARRAMÁN: I am Escarramán,[68] so pay attention:
Here's a brief account of my long history.

      SECOND MUSICIAN *returns with two guitars and*
      gives one to his companion.

The galley ran aground on Barbary shore,
And since a heartless judge had sentenced me
To ply an oar and set the pace for others,
There I was with my fellows in the stern,[69]
This change of fortune left me captive still,

For I was now the slave of Turkish masters.
Two months later, with Heaven's gracious blessing,
I made off with a galley and escaped,
Regaining freedom and my independence.
I took a vow and made a solemn promise
That I would wear these clothes and bear this chain
Till I reached home. Once there I'd hang them on
The sacred walls of that most holy place
That's known as San Millán de la Cogolla.[70]
So now you've heard the strange and wondrous story
That's worthy to be treasured in my memory.
My woman Méndez, has she lost her looks?
Does she still live?

JUAN: Right royally in Granada!

CHIQUIZNAQUE: It seems the poor man is quite lovesick still!

ESCARRAMÁN: What did they say about me in this world,
    While in the other one I was detained
    By fortune and misfortunes?

MOSTRENCA: Much was said:
    On stage they've often acted out your hanging.

PIZPITA: The urchins turned you inside out and made
    A proper hotch-potch of your various parts.

REPULIDA: You've become a saint: what more do you want?

CHIQUIZNAQUE: They sing about you in the streets and
                                                    squares;
    They dance to you in theatres and at home;
    You've kept the poets busier than Virgil,
    When he set down in verse the fall of Troy!

JUAN: Your name resounds in taverns and in inns.

REPULIDA: Kitchen maids sing your praises by the river,
    Stable boys strum them on their currycombs.

CHIQUIZNAQUE: Tanners use their shears to serenade you –
    You're far more famous than the old grey mare.[71]

MOSTRENCA: Blow by blow your fame has reached the
                                                    Indies;[72]
    In Rome your misadventures are well known;
    They've worn their boots out tapping out your measure.

VADEMECUM: God's truth, they've pounded you like
                                                    peppercorns,
    And left you like a crushed and fading flower.
    You used to be so sharp – no flies on you;

And now you're merely flyblown, even snotty.[73]
Of all the fancy dances now in fashion
(The competition's tough and quite relentless)
It's yours that wins the day and wears the crown.

ESCARRAMÁN: Let me be famous, I'll not mind the tatters,
  I'd even burn a temple if I had to.[74]

    The MUSICIANS improvise a tune and begin to sing
    a ballad.

MUSICIANS: Fresh from the galleys he returns,
             Escarramán the fearless lad,
             To terrify our local coppers
             And change his lot to good from bad.

ESCARRAMÁN: Is that an invitation, may I ask?
  You think I take no further joy in pleasure?
  Well, now I'm lighter than I was before,
  So play away and let's roll up our sleeves.[75]

PIZPITA: No one can match you when it comes to dancing!
  You're just as good as ever!

VADEMECUM: Lithe and limber!

JUAN: He can dance to celebrate Trampagos's wedding.

ESCARRAMÁN: Strike up! You'll see I'm made of pure
                               quicksilver.

MUSICIANS: Take your cue for dancing from my song,
  And so avoid confusion and disorder.

ESCARRAMÁN: Strike up! I can't keep still a moment longer!

REPULIDA: I long to see him enter the affray.

MUSICIANS: Take your places everyone.

CHIQUIZNAQUE: We're ready.

         (*They sing.*)
      Fresh from the galleys he returns,
      Escarramán, the fearless lad,
      To terrify the local coppers
      And change his luck to good from bad.
      He's back again to show the world
      His sleight-of-hand and nimble skill,
      Agility and dashing charm:
      His Majesty is with us still.
      Since Coscolina[76] can't be here,
      Let Repulida lead the throng –
      She smells as sweet as orange flowers;

> While our Pizpita clears her throat,
> Escarramán will deftly show
> Us how the Galliard should go.
> (*They play music for a Galliard.* ESCARRAMÁN *dances
> it and after the opening the ballad continues.*)
> Now Repulida takes the floor
> To dance the lively Rastreado,[77]
> She was the first to demonstrate
> It here for us with great bravado.
> Escarramán will partner her;
> Pizpita also shows her talent
> Chiquiznaque and Mostrenca,
> With Juan Claros, the handsome gallant!
> Hallelujah, it's going so smoothly!
> You couldn't ask for greater pleasure,
> Or greater skill and elegance,
> Or better stepping to the measure!
> Go to it, friends, don't miss a beat,
> Oh happy band of pimps and whores!
> No other libertines you know
> Are more deserving of applause.
> Ah, see those drooping, languid hands!
> Such advancing and retreating
> In unsuspected labyrinths,
> Couples parting and then meeting.
> Whatever dance may take their fancy,
> With our music we can follow,
> The Canario or Gameta,
> Zarabanda, Zambapalo,
> Rustic Villano or, perhaps,
> The Mournful Trot or something lewd,
> Like that old chestnut honouring
> Worthy King Alonso the Good.

ESCARRAMÁN: If you're playing the Canario,
I mean to dance it all alone.

MUSICIANS: Although we'll play with all our skill,
Your dancing fairly takes the prize.

> (*They play the Canario,* ESCARRAMÁN *dances it
> by himself. After they finish, he speaks.*)

ESCARRAMÁN: Let's dance the rustic Villano,
Not forgetting all the verses.

You three musicians, play the tune.

MUSICIANS: St John grant you tender mercies!
  (*They dance the Villano energetically. After that,*
  ESCARRAMÁN *can ask for whatever dance he wants.*
  Finally, TRAMPAGOS *speaks.*)

TRAMPAGOS: Our celebrations have outdone
  Those of Roland[78] in the legend.
  So let us join and say as one,
  Long live our friend Escarramán!

EVERYONE: Long live Escarramán!

CAST

THE ELECTION OF THE
MAGISTRATES OF DAGANZO

BACHELOR HOOF
PETER SNEEZE
CRUSTY
ALONSO STRINGBEAN
JOHNNY CLOD
FRANCIS PUFF
MICHAEL KNUCKLEKNEES
PETER FROG
A MAN
MUSICIANS
TWO GYPSY GIRLS
SEXTON

THE ELECTION OF THE MAGISTRATES
OF DAGANZO

(La elección de los alcaldes de Daganzo)[79]

Enter BACHELOR HOOF; PETER SNEEZE, *notary*;
CRUSTY *and* ALONSO STRINGBEAN, *aldermen*.

CRUSTY: Let's take our ease, for all will turn out well
  If blessed Heaven wills it should be so.

STRINGBEAN: Let's raise the roof. The devil take the rest!

CRUSTY: Don't fret my friend. If Heaven smiles on us,
  We'll do ourselves quite well in this affair.

STRINGBEAN: Let Heaven smile or not – it's in our hands.

CRUSTY: See here, Stringbean, your tongue is running wild!
  Speak properly and mind your Ps and Qs:
  I do not like the sound of what you've said:
  'Let Heaven smile or not': my sainted aunt!
  Evidently you think you know it all,
  And throw yourself full tilt into the fray.

STRINGBEAN: My blood is purest Christian through and
                                        through
  And my belief in God unflinching.

BACHELOR HOOF: Good!
  Nothing could be better.

STRINGBEAN: So if by chance
  I put it badly, I admit my folly,
  The note I struck was sour, I'm just a goose;
  Let's pretend I never said it.

NOTARY: Enough!
  God shows mercy to the worst offender,
  If he repents his sins.

STRINGBEAN: Then I declare
  That I repent and shall be saved. I know
  That Heaven chooses what it wants to do
  And no one gives it orders or dictates,
  Above all when it rains.

CRUSTY: Hold on, Stringbean,
  The rain falls from the clouds and not from Heaven!

STRINGBEAN: God's teeth! If we have gathered here today
   To criticise and call each other names,
   Then let's admit it. Let the brickbats fall
   On Stringbean's clumsy head wherever he turns.
BACHELOR HOOF: 'Redeamus ad rem': as we were saying,[80]
   Crusty and Stringbean, if you'll pay attention,
   Let's not waste time in childishness and quibbling.
   You say our meeting's marred with idle squabble,
   But every time your paths just chance to cross,
   Countless storms and squalls break out between you,
   As each one tries to contradict the other.
NOTARY: The worthy graduate puts it very well;
   But now let's turn to matters that are pressing:
   We must ensure the magistrates we choose
   For office in the coming year are such
   That our most noble masters in Toledo
   Will give their blessing and confirm our choice.[81]
   That is the reason why we've gathered here.
CRUSTY: There are four claimants to the staff of office.
   Their names are Johnny Clod and Francis Puff,
   With Michael Knuckleknees and Peter Frog:
   All men of stature, wise and sound in judgement,
   Worthy not just to govern in Daganzo,
   But also in Rome.
STRINGBEAN: Or closer to home![82]
NOTARY: Any more observations? By St Nick,
   I'm leaving if you don't stop butting in!
STRINGBEAN: The notary is well named Mr Sneeze,
   For every puff of smoke goes to his head.
   But calm yourself, I'll not say any more.
CRUSTY: Can such be found in all this blessed sorbet?
STRINGBEAN: What blessed sorbet? Orbit is the word
   That Mr Crusty seeks in all his wisdom.[83]
CRUSTY: What I mean to say is it's not possible
   In all the world you'd find such clever men
   As our four candidates.
STRINGBEAN: At least it's true
   That our good Mr Clod has the finest
   Instinct.
NOTARY: For what?
STRINGBEAN: For judging wine, y'know,

His taste's unerring: none can equal him.
Why, just the other day he tried some wine
I had at home. He told me that it tasted
Of wood and iron and leather. When the jar
Was drained, imagine what it still contained:
A piece of wood, from which there hung a strap
Of kidskin, and on that a tiny key![84]

NOTARY: What rare ability! What genius!
Someone so gifted is cut out to govern
Towns like Esquivias, famous for their wine![85]

STRINGBEAN: That Knuckleknees is an eagle.

BACHELOR HOOF: How's that?

STRINGBEAN: When he hunts for birds with his catapult.

BACHELOR HOOF: Is his aim so good?

STRINGBEAN: So good, indeed,
That if more of his shots managed to land
On their mark and not in his other hand,
No birds would be heard in this neighbourhood.

BACHELOR HOOF: That skill is needed in a magistrate!

STRINGBEAN: What shall I say about our Francis Puff?
He mends a shoe as well as any tailor.
And Peter Frog – his memory's prodigious.
No one can touch him: he'll recall at will,
And word for word, that famous ode or ditty
About the dog that barked so much in Alba.[86]

CRUSTY: He has my vote!

NOTARY: And I'll choose him as well!

STRINGBEAN: I'll vote for Mr Clod.

BACHELOR HOOF: And I for none!
They have to prove their skill and *savoir-faire*
In matters of jurisprudence and the like.

STRINGBEAN: There's a solution for that, so I propose
The candidates present themselves before us
And Bachelor Hoof will cross-examine them
(He's qualified and knows a thing or two).
That way we'll find the best man for the job.

NOTARY: God bless us, what an unusual plan!

CRUSTY: This idea could well be recommended
To His Majesty; just as the Court is filled
With impotent doctors, let us fill our town
With impotent magistrates!

STRINGBEAN: You mean to say
  'Important', Crusty, never 'impotent'![87]
CRUSTY: You talk just like a legal persecutor.
STRINGBEAN: 'Prosecutor', if you don't mind . . .
NOTARY: My word,
  Mr Stringbean has quite a nerve!
STRINGBEAN: I say
  That since there are exams to qualify
  For barbers, smiths and tailors (surgeons, too),
  With other riff-raff, then we should require
  That magistrates submit to scrutiny.
  Those who qualify for such an office
  Should then receive a letter of approval
  Of which the candidate can make good use.
  Tucking his hard-won credentials in a tube
  Of shiny tin secured across his chest.[88]
  The wretch would make his way to some small town
  Willing to pay him twice his weight in gold.
  Such towns exist today which sorely lack
  For magistrates both wise and also clever.
BACHELOR HOOF: That is well said. The reasoning is shrewd.
  So let's have Clod come in and we shall see
  How far the brilliance of his mind can reach.
STRINGBEAN: Well, here they come, our worthy candidates:
  Puff and Frog, with Clod and Knuckleknees.
                    Enter four labourers.
    And now they've arrived.
BACHELOR HOOF: Welcome, gentlemen.
CLOD: We trust we find you blooming, gentlemen.
CRUSTY: Do take a seat. There are no end of chairs.
PUFF: I'll take a seat, although I'm quite upset.
KNUCKLEKNEES: We'll all be seated, may the Lord be praised.
FROG: Why are you so upset, Puff?
PUFF: It's because
  Our election is so endlessly delayed.
  Must we offer turkeys, or cows with young,
  Pitchers of honey and skins of vintage wine
  Filled full to bursting and stretched beyond their size?
  Just say the word and it can soon be done.
BACHELOR HOOF: Bribes are out of the question here! We're
                                                            all

Agreed and of one mind in this affair:
Whoever seems best fitted for the job
Can count on our approval and election.
FROG: That sounds all right to me. I'm satisfied.
CLOD: Me too.
BACHELOR HOOF: That's excellent and welcome news!
PUFF: I'm satisfied as well.
KNUCKLEKNEES: It's to my liking.
BACHELOR HOOF: Let us proceed with our questions.
PUFF: Fire
                                                away!

BACHELOR HOOF: Puff, can you read?
PUFF: What do you take me
                                                for?

There's not a trace in my whole ancestry
Of anyone who showed so little sense
As those who study all that empty moonshine:
Such men most often end up on the bonfire,
And women in a house of ill-repute.[89]
I cannot read but what I know instead
Is far more useful than a load of books!
BACHELOR HOOF: Give an example.
PUFF: I have learned by heart
The Paternoster and three other prayers
And I recite them several times a week.[90]
FROG: You think with that they'll make you a magistrate?
PUFF: With that and because I'm Christian through and
                                            through
I'd dare to be a Roman senator.
BACHELOR HOOF: That's good enough. It's your turn,
                                        Knuckleknees,
To tell us what you know.
KNUCKLEKNEES: Well, Mr Hoof,
I can read a bit. I know the letters –
I've spent the last three months among the Bs –
In another five I'll have them polished off.
Along with this new learning I am able
To sharpen ploughshares to a fine perfection;
Give me four pairs of wild unbroken oxen,
Within three hours I'll have them branded for you.
I'm sound in all my parts; free from deafness,

Cataracts, rheumatics and bronchitis.
I'm a true Christian like the others here
And handy with a bow as any Roman.[91]

STRINGBEAN: Unusual talents for a magistrate!
So varied and so useful!

BACHELOR HOOF: Let's continue.
What can Clod do?

CLOD: All my skills and talents
Lie in my tongue as well as in my throat:
You'll never meet a better judge of wine.
Sixty-six flavours are stamped on my palate,
And every one is vinicultural!

STRINGBEAN: You want to be a magistrate?

CLOD: Most surely.
For when I've sacrificed at Bacchus' shrine
My senses seem to sharpen and I dream
Lycurgus asks me what is what in law
And then I wipe my arse with legal texts.[92]

CRUSTY: Mind what you say when Council is in session!

CLOD: I'm not a prude, but neither am I boorish:
I simply say I'd better get my due,
Or else I promise you I'll raise the devil.

BACHELOR HOOF: So you would threaten us? Upon my life,
Good Mr Clod, those threats won't get you far!
Peter Frog, what do you say?

FROG: I'm bound
Like any frog, to sing quite wretchedly;
So I'll speak of my condition, not my wit.
I'll tell you how I am, and nothing else.
If I'm elected magistrate, good sirs,
My rod of office won't be just a twig;
I'll choose a sturdy oak and cut a branch
As thick as two good fingers, taking care
That it not bend beneath the honeyed weight
Of purses full of ducats and the like:
Of supplications, promises and favours
That weigh like lead, yet seem as light as air
Until they crush and bruise you, body and soul.
Apart from that, I'll practise moderation,
And temper firmness with a gentle hand.
I'll never shame the poor unhappy creature

Whose crimes I find myself obliged to hear;
A judge's thoughtless words will often punish
More than the sentence that a man must serve.
For power should not diminish courtesy;
No judge should take advantage of his prisoner
And pride himself to see another brought low.

STRINGBEAN: Praise be to God, just listen to our Frog!
He sings far better than a dying swan!

CRUSTY: His words are worthy of the Roman censor.

STRINGBEAN: You mean the noble Cato.[93] That's well said,
Alderman Crusty . . .

CRUSTY: Go on, set me right!

STRINGBEAN: Your time will come, sir.

NOTARY: That will never be.
Mr Stringbean, you have a dreadful habit
Of setting people right.

STRINGBEAN: Enough said, scribbler.

NOTARY: How's that, pharisee?[94]

BACHELOR HOOF: By great St Peter,
That's going much too far!

STRINGBEAN: Of course I'm joking!

NOTARY: And so am I.

BACHELOR HOOF: Then stop your jokes, I beg you.

STRINGBEAN: It's clear who's lying.

NOTARY: And who's telling the
                                            truth.

STRINGBEAN: That's true.

NOTARY: Be sure to mind your own business
                                            too!

PUFF: Those promises Frog made are unconvincing
And too remote. But once he grabs the rod
Of office, watch him change his tune. He'll be
A different man from now.

BACHELOR HOOF: What Puff has said
Is apropos . . .

PUFF: And I would add a thought:
That if you give the rod to me, you'll see
That I won't budge, or move or change.

BACHELOR HOOF: Well, here you have the rod. You may
                                            consider
Yourself elected magistrate.

STRINGBEAN: God's teeth!
  You've slipped him a left-handed rod?
PUFF: What's that?
STRINGBEAN: Well, isn't it left-handed? It's quite clear
  To everyone, even the deaf and mute.
PUFF: How can I use a rod that seems left-handed
  And still gives justice that is right?
NOTARY: The devil
  Is in that Stringbean's tongue! Now have you ever
  Seen such things as rods that are left-handed!
                 A MAN *enters.*
MAN: I bring good news, the gypsies have arrived,
  Together with some lovely gypsy girls.
  They know your worships are engaged in business
  But still insist they must be given leave
  To entertain your worships.
BACHELOR HOOF: Let them in.
  Perhaps they'll help us all to celebrate
  The feast of Corpus, which is in my charge.[95]
CRUSTY: They'll be very welcome.
BACHELOR HOOF: Bring them in.
PUFF: I'm all in favour!
KNUCKLEKNEES: Count me in as well!
FROG: You say they're gypsies? We must take good care
  Or else they'll rob us blind.
MAN: Well, here they are.
  They've walked right in without a by-you-leave.
        Enter MUSICIANS *dressed as gypsies, with two*
        GYPSY GIRLS *in fine clothes. They dance as*
        the MUSICIANS *sing a ballad.*
      Good councillors of Daganzo,
      We greet each one with reverent bow.
      Quite suddenly you're men of worth:
      Wisdom and judgement crown your brow,
      Fitting you for any office
      A Moor or Christian might occupy.
      Heaven has surely smiled upon you,
      Set you as stars to light the sky:
      Samsons of knowledge, learning and wit,
      And Solomons of muscle and grit.[96]

KNUCKLEKNEES: There's truth in every word those folks are
                                                     singing.

PUFF: They really have no sequel anywhere.

STRINGBEAN: You could say without equal . . .[97]

BACHELOR HOOF: That's
                                                  enough!

MUSICIANS: As breezes shift and branches change,
                  From leafless winter to budding spring,
                  As women choose then change their mind –
                  And no one stops to think it strange,
                  We too will vary step with step,
                  And quickly demonstrate our range.
                  Councillors, may you live many days,
                  Solid as oak and worthy of praise.
                        (*They dance.*)

KNUCKLEKNEES: What excellent verses!

PUFF: So deeply felt!

CLOD: They should be published as fitting monument
   To us for all the ages yet to come.

BACHELOR HOOF: I wish they'd stop their chatter and be
                                                     quiet!

MUSICIANS: As the centuries fly by,
                  Swift as birds on the wing,
                  May they flourish untouched
                  By the blemish of time –
                  As stout and as sturdy
                  As their ancient cork trees!
                  Whenever they venture
                  To set sail on the seas,
                  May temperate breezes
                  Blow soft in their faces!
                  Councillors, may you live many days,
                  Solid as oak and worthy of praise.

BACHELOR HOOF: I'm not so sure the chorus pleases me,
   But, on the whole, it's good . . .

CLOD: So let's hear more.

MUSICIANS: I'll trip the light fantastic
                  As often as I please.
                  I'll set the dust a-flying
                  As often as I may.[98]

CRUSTY: What a proper hash these musicians make

Of what they sing!

PUFF: What devils gypsies are!

MUSICIANS: I'll set the dust a-flying –
                    However hard the floor,
                    For that is where my heart
                    Lies buried and entombed:
                    All my happiness
                    Was trampled on by Love. –
                    As often as I may
                    I'll trip my merry way –
                    No matter what the pain,
                    And even if my love
                    Is trampled underfoot;
                    My joy has flown away,
                    Leaving a taste of dust –
                    As often as I may.

                Enter a shabbily dressed UNDER-SEXTON.

SEXTON: God bless my soul, good sirs, what's this I see?
     Surely you know that leisure does great harm!
     Is this the way the town is to be run,
     With music, dancing and such sinful pleasures?

BACHELOR HOOF: Grab him, Kunuckleknees!

KNUCKLEKNEES: Nothing could
                                    be simpler!

                (They catch hold of him.)

BACHELOR HOOF: Bring a blanket here. Upon my life,
     We're going to treat this wretch to such a tossing!
     He's stupid and shameless and impertinent,
     As well as much too bold.

SEXTON: Now hear me, sirs . . .

STRINGBEAN: Quick as a wink I'll have that blanket here!
                                    [*He exits.*]

SEXTON: I'll have you know I've taken holy orders.

BACHELOR HOOF: How's that, you worm? What orders, may I
                                        ask?

SEXTON: I've had my head shaved once, that's much the
                                    same.[99]

CRUSTY: To quote the good knight: 'We'll see what we shall
                                    see . . .'[100]

SEXTON: I see no good knights here!

BACHELOR HOOF: Good night's what you'll
                                                    say
When we have finished what we have in mind!
FROG: Tell me, unhappy man, just what possessed you
   And made you speak as if you were the judge?
   Are you elected here to be a governor?
   Keep to your bells and mind your special duties.[101]
   Leave governing to others better trained
   For what they have to do than all of us.
   If they are bad, then pray for their improvement;
   And if they're good, then pray they'll long be with us!
BACHELOR HOOF: Our Frog is no less than a blessed saint!
                    STRINGBEAN *returns with a blanket.*
STRINGBEAN: The blanket's here.
BACHELOR HOOF: Let everyone take hold
   Of it – that means our gypsy minstrels too!
   All together, friends!
SEXTON: Good grief, I'm for it!
   God knows I'm hopping mad, for who am I
   To put up with these jokes? By great St Peter,
   I'll excommunicate each one of you
   Who's dared to lay a hand upon this blanket![102]
FROG: Enough. No more. This punishment must stop.
   The poor man must be sorry for his words.
SEXTON: Indeed, I'm quite worn out; so from now on
   I'll keep my lips stitched tight as if with thread . . .
FROG: That's what we want to hear.
BACHELOR HOOF: A word with you,
   Good gypsy friends. Come to my house.
GYPSIES: Agreed.
BACHELOR HOOF: The election's postponed until tomorrow,
                                                    when
   I here declare my vote will be for Frog.
GYPSIES: Now shall we sing, sir?
BACHELOR HOOF: That is as you please.
CRUSTY: No one sings as well as our own Frog.
KNUCKLEKNEES: It isn't just his pleasant voice
   That makes him seem the obvious choice.
                    [*Exit all, singing 'I'll trip the light fantastic . . .'*]

SIR VIGILANT

INTRODUCTION

The two protagonists in this piece have much in common with two well-known comic types, the braggart soldier of Roman Comedy and the venal sexton of early Castilian farce. A contest between rival suitors is also a familiar comic situation in Italian literature.[103] The structure of the dialogue, in which the two suitors trade insults, is reminiscent of Lope de Rueda's *Pasos*. Yet all these stereotypes take on distinctive characteristics and this gives the piece freshness and originality.

Although we are never told the soldier's name, we learn a good deal about him: for example, that he has fought in Italy and visited Portugal, and that he has been in Madrid little more than a month. A knowing audience or contemporary reader would no doubt identify him with one of the countless Spaniards who returned from fighting for their country to find themselves forgotten and marginalised. Like Cervantes himself, the soldier hopes for eventual recognition: he boasts of his expectations of being given a command in Naples or appointed 'custodian of a famous castle'. True to the times, as well, are the references to the interminable, futile bureaucracy: the soldier offers to show Cristina's master a bundle of documents with reports on his military service and recommendations from his superiors;[104] he has also petitioned the king 'with a list of my past services and present needs'. As a measure of his devotion to Cristina (as well as a further indication of his poverty) he writes her a love letter on the back of this petition.

Despite the soldier's ridiculous posturing and exaggeration, his successful rival is scarcely more attractive. Yet it is not difficult to see why, in the world of the Interlude, Cristina chooses the sexton. As the soldier ruefully acknowledges in the final song:

> A ragged soldier cannot match
> A sexton's higher bid for favour,

> For when it comes to love or cash,
> She'll choose the cash and never waver.

Cristina is a realist, not a romantic. The soldier may promise her a castle, but that is nothing but air compared with the reality of what the sexton has to offer:

> There isn't a sexton to touch me when it comes to
> arranging funerals or decorating the church for a
> solemn occasion. I can still carry out those duties
> when I'm married, so we'll eat like kings.

Beside the central trio of characters, there is a procession of minor figures: a young boy begging alms to take care of a shrine; a Portuguese peddler; a shoemaker with an admiration for Lope de Vega; the sexton's belligerent friend, Grajales; Cristina's employers, with their concern for their servant's virtue and marriage prospects; the barber's apprentices who serve as musicians at the end of the play: all add colourful touches to this miniature of life in seventeenth-century Madrid.

CAST

SOLDIER
SEXTON PASILLAS
FIRST BOY
SECOND BOY
CRISTINA
SHOEMAKER
CRISTINA'S MASTER
SEXTON GRAJALES
CRISTINA'S MISTRESS
MUSICIANS

SIR VIGILANT

(La guarda cuidadosa)

A SOLDIER *enters, dressed in rags, with a threadbare military sash and a tube containing documents across his chest.*[105] *A sickly looking* SEXTON *follows him.*

SOLDIER: Why do you follow me, man, like a lost soul?

SEXTON: I'm no lost soul. I'm solid flesh and blood.

SOLDIER: That may be so. Still, my misfortune compels me to ask who you are and what business you have in this street.

SEXTON: My good fortune compels me to reply that my name is Lorenzo Pasillas. I'm under-sexton and jack-of-all-trades in this parish.[106] My business in this street is the same as yours, but I have better prospects than you.

SOLDIER: So you're looking for Cristinica, the kitchen maid who lives in this house?

SEXTON: If you say so.

SOLDIER: Well, come over here, you devil's jackass.

SEXTON: At your service, you renegade knave.

SOLDIER: Stand a little closer.

Me and you . . . what a crew!

Knave and Jack . . . what a pack!

Give us a king and we'd have a full house![107]

I told you to come here, Pasillas my friend, so I can run you through with my pikestaff. Don't you know that Cristinica is mine?

SEXTON: Don't you know, scarecrow, that I've already bid on that piece of baggage? What's more, my price is right!

SOLDIER: God's blood! I swear I'll run you through and through, I'll leave your head full of holes.

SEXTON: Never mind my head. Look to the holes in your own breeches!

SOLDIER: Have you ever spoken to Cristina?

SEXTON: I speak to her whenever I please.

SOLDIER: What gifts have you bestowed on her?

SEXTON: Heaps of them.

SOLDIER: How many? Tell me what they were.

SEXTON: I gave her a quince-jelly box filled with snowy white wafers left over from the Mass.[108] To these I added four wax-candle stubs – whiter than ermine they were, too.

SOLDIER: What else have you given her?

SEXTON: A letter promising to serve her in a thousand different ways.

SOLDIER: How has she answered you?

SEXTON: I have reason to believe that she will soon become my wife.

SOLDIER: So you haven't yet taken your vow of celibacy?

SEXTON: Far from it! I may be a bit thin on top, but I can marry whenever I please.[109] You'll see soon enough.

SOLDIER: Just a minute, you hairless wretch. Answer me this: if the wench truly welcomes your attentions – which I doubt, considering how paltry your gifts are – how do you think she'll reward my generosity? Only the other day I sent her a letter, professing my love, written on the back of a petition to His Majesty, no less, with a list of my past services and present needs. (As a soldier I'm not ashamed to admit I'm poor.) My petition was approved and sent to the Royal almsgiver for prompt attention. So you see, I didn't give a thought to the value of that piece of paper. Instead, with a nonchalance and generosity that astound even me, I scribbled my note on the back of it.

> This done, my sullied heart can better rest,
> For by her saintly hand the note's possessed.

SEXTON: What else have you sent her?

SOLDIER: Sighs, sulks, sobs, palpitations and weak knees – the whole pack of tricks that lovers use to declare their passion.

SEXTON: Have you serenaded her?

SOLDIER: Only with the music of my sighs.

SEXTON: Well, I've often shaken the town sleepless with an incessant ringing of bells. I do it to please her and to let her know that I'm in the belltower at her service. When I have to toll for a funeral I jangle the bells merrily at Vespers.

SOLDIER: There you have the advantage of me, for I've nothing of value to jangle.

SEXTON: How does Cristina repay your attentions?

SOLDIER: She refuses to see me. She won't even speak to me.

She curses if she passes me in the street, and dumps the slops on my head when she finishes washing the clothes and mopping the floor. This happens daily, since I spend all my time in the street at her door. I'm Sir Vigilant; I'm her watchdog, she's my manger – if I can't lie in her then no one else shall![110] So, Mr Jack-of-all-trades, be off. It's only respect for your holy calling that has kept me from tearing you to shreds.[111]

SEXTON: I'd be in a sorry state if I looked like those shreds of yours!

SOLDIER: A monk is more than the habit he wears. A soldier who loses everything in war is like a student whose ragged cloak proclaims him a veteran at his studies. Now get out of here or I'll be as good as my word.

SEXTON: It's easy to threaten while I'm unarmed. Just wait here, Sir Vigilant, and we'll see who calls the tune.

SOLDIER: Should I be afraid of someone whose name suggests a shrivelled prune?[112]

SEXTON: 'We'll see what we shall see.'[113]

[*Exit the* SEXTON]

SOLDIER: Aaaah, women, women! What fickle, capricious creatures! Cristina, how can you ignore this paragon of the military profession and settle for that jackass of an undersexton? Why, if you wanted, you could get yourself a full-fledged sexton, or even a canon. I'll do my best to spoil your pleasure. I'll stand at your door and chase your suitors away. I'll live up to the name of Sir Vigilant.

Enter *a young* BOY, *dressed in green and carrying a begging box, like those who seek alms for a sacred image.*[114]

FIRST BOY: For the love of God, give alms to keep the lamp burning on St Lucy's shrine, so she'll keep your eyes from harm. Is anyone at home? Can you spare a coin?

SOLDIER: Greetings, my sainted young friend! Come over here. What do you want in this house?

FIRST BOY: Can't you see, sir? Alms for St Lucy's lamp.

SOLDIER: For the lamp or for oil to put in it? Your meaning's not clear.

FIRST BOY: Everyone knows it's for oil to put *in* the lamp.

SOLDIER: Do they usually give you something in this house?

FIRST BOY: Two farthings a day.

SOLDIER: Who gives them to you?

FIRST BOY: Whoever's around, but it's usually the little kitchen maid Cristina – she's a jewel.

SOLDIER: The little kitchen maid is a jewel?

FIRST BOY: A real pearl!

SOLDIER: So, she doesn't displease you?

FIRST BOY: I'd be a block of wood if she did!

SOLDIER: What's your name? I can't keep calling you my sainted young friend.

FIRST BOY: My name's Andrew, sir.

SOLDIER: Well, Master Andrew, just listen to what I have to say: here are eight farthings – take note that I'm paying you four days' advance for the alms you usually receive from Cristina. And God speed you. Just remember, if you dare come near this house in the next four days I'll take my boot to your behind.

FIRST BOY: Don't you worry, sir. I'm leaving right away and I'll not be back this month.

[*Exit* FIRST BOY]

SOLDIER: On guard, Sir Vigilant. There's no rest for you!
Enter ANOTHER BOY *calling out his wares: braided hair ribbons, lengths of fine Cambray cloth, Flemish lace, and Portuguese cotton.*[115]

SECOND BOY: Come buy! Come buy! I have ribbons for your hair, fine French cloth and Flemish lace, the best Portuguese cotton.

(CRISTINA *leans out of the window*.)

CRISTINA: I'm glad to see you, Manuel! Have you brought us some trimmings for shirts?

SECOND BOY: Yes, I have – of the best quality.

CRISTINA: Come in then, my mistress is waiting for them.

SOLDIER: Ah, my ill-fated lodestar, you lure me to destruction! Mr Hair-ribbon, or whatever your name is, do you know that young lady who just called you from the window?

SECOND BOY: Of course I know her. What's that to you, sir?

SOLDIER: Does she not have a fair face and a graceful manner?

SECOND BOY: That goes without saying!

SOLDIER: It also goes without saying that you're not entering that house! If you do, then by God, I'll break every bone in your body!

SECOND BOY: You mean I can't go in even though they're waiting to buy my wares?

SOLDIER: Begone, not a word more, or I'll carry out my threat in short order!

SECOND BOY: It's not fair ... take it easy, mister soldier, I'm going, I'm going.

[*Exit* MANUEL. CRISTINA *leans out of the window.*]

CRISTINA: Manuel ... Where are you?

SOLDIER: Manuel just left, my lady of the trimmings.[116]

CRISTINA: Dear Lord, what a tiresome brute! You down there! What are you doing at our door?

[*Exit* CRISTINA]

SOLDIER: My sun withdrew behind the clouds
                And left the earth in darkest shrouds.

Enter a SHOEMAKER, *carrying a small pair of new slippers. As he approaches* CRISTINA's *door, the* SOLDIER *stops him.*

SOLDIER: One moment, sir. Do you have business in this house?

SHOEMAKER: Indeed I have.

SOLDIER: Who with, may I ask?

SHOEMAKER: I'm looking for a certain kitchen maid who lives here. I've brought her these slippers she ordered.

SOLDIER: So your honour is a shoemaker?

SHOEMAKER: I've fitted her many times.

SOLDIER: And have you come to fit her now?

SHOEMAKER: There's no need. I only do that when she orders a pair of boots.

SOLDIER: These slippers, have they been paid for?

SHOEMAKER: No, not yet. I expect her to pay me today.

SOLDIER: Will you do me a great favour, sir? Trust me with these slippers and I'll give you something of equal value as security. Just until the day after tomorrow when I'll have plenty of money to buy them off you.

SHOEMAKER: I'm willing, but first I want to see what you're giving me as security. I'm a penniless craftsman and I don't trust anyone.

SOLDIER: I'm giving you a toothpick that I prize highly. Believe me, I wouldn't sell it to you for any money. Tell me where I can find your shop, sir, when I'm ready to redeem it.

SHOEMAKER: I own one of those stalls on the High Street. My name's Jack Straw.[117]

SOLDIER: Well, Mr Straw, here's the toothpick. Mind you treat it with respect, for nothing means more to me.

SHOEMAKER: Why, it's just an ordinary stick, not worth two farthings! How can you expect me to treat it with respect, sir?

SOLDIER: God strike me dead! I only gave it to you as a reminder for myself, so that when I find it's not in my pocket I'll remember I have to redeem it from you. Take my word as a soldier that I have no other reason to give it to you. Still, if you're not satisfied, I'll throw in this sash and document tube as well. After all, an honest man is not afraid to give pledges.

SHOEMAKER: I'm just a poor shoemaker, but I'm not so churlish as to deprive your honour of your precious possessions. You must hold on to them and I'll hold on to my slippers – that's what suits me best.

SOLDIER: What size are the slippers?

SHOEMAKER: Small enough.

SOLDIER: But not small enough for my purse. My beloved slippers, I can't raise six shillings to pay for you! Listen, my worthy friend, I'd like to improvise a poem for you on the subject of 'My beloved slippers'.

SHOEMAKER: Is your honour a poet?

SOLDIER: A famous one, as you shall hear. Just listen to this:

> O my beloved slippers.
> Love is such a jealous brute,
> Treating my sighs with lordly scorn;
> Now with this suitor for her foot,
> He kills my hopes so newly born
> And to my claim he gives the boot.
> These are your exploits, slippery pair,
> Turning my dreams to emptiest air.
> But since to Cristina I know you belong
> I cannot refrain from addressing this song
> To my beloved slippers.

SHOEMAKER: Poetry isn't my strong point, but these verses strike me as worthy of great Lope himself . . . like everything else that's considered good around here.[118]

SOLDIER: Well, sir, since you're not willing to trust me with the slippers – not even in return for my precious pledges – take the toothpick anyway. At the very least, keep the slippers until I come for them in two days. Until then, Mr Shoemaker, mind you stay away from Cristina.

SHOEMAKER: I'll do what you ask, my soldier friend, for I can tell the shoe pinches in two places – in your pocket and your pride.

SOLDIER: What a genius! This shoemaker must have graduated with distinction.[119]

SHOEMAKER: Ah, jealousy, jealousy – the green-eyed monster that leads to certain grief.

[*Exit the* SHOEMAKER]

SOLDIER: Not if you keep careful watch, Sir Vigilant:

> Buzzing and swarming come the flies
> To the cellar where your best wine lies!

But wait, whose voice is that? Surely that's my Cristina. She always sings while she does her work.

(*From within* CRISTINA *sings as she
washes dishes.*)

CRISTINA:

> The sexton's the love of my life
> I'll always be constant and true,
> And make him a wonderful wife,
> So sing alelu, alelu!

SOLDIER: Will you listen to that! There's no doubt the sexton's wormed his way into her favour.

> Ah, my queen of dishwashers,
> The fairest of your kind,
> Scrubbing at the pots and pans
> Till they all are shined.
> While you clean the dirty dishes,
> Washing off their stain,
> Why not purge your immodest wishes
> And wash your sexton down the drain?

Enter CRISTINA'*s* MASTER.

MASTER: What do you want here, young man? Are you looking for something?

SOLDIER: I want more than's good for me and I'm looking for something I can't find. Who are you and what business is it of yours?

MASTER: I'm the master of this house.

SOLDIER: Cristinica's master?

MASTER: The very same.

SOLDIER: Well, sir, just you come over here and take this bundle of papers. Look inside. You'll find reports on my military service, with recommendations signed by twenty-two generals under whose standards I've served, plus thirty-four more from field marshals who've been good enough to give me their support.

MASTER: As far as I know, there haven't been that number of generals or field marshals in the Spanish infantry for the past hundred years!

SOLDIER: You're a man of peace, sir, and not expected to be an expert on the subject of warfare. Take a glance at these documents and you'll find every single general and field marshal I've mentioned.

MASTER: I'll take your word for it – but why should I be concerned?

SOLDIER: I'll have you know I've almost certainly been recommended for one of three vacant commands in Naples: that's to say, either in Gaeta, Barleta or Reggio Calabria.[120]

MASTER: So far, nothing you've told me matters one jot to me.

SOLDIER: God willing, I know that it *will* matter to you.

MASTER: How can that be?

SOLDIER: Unless the sky falls on our heads, I'll be appointed to one of those commands, so I want to marry Cristinica right away. When I'm her husband, then you, sir, may dispose of my person and my not inconsiderable fortune as if they were your own. I'll not show myself ungrateful for the careful upbringing my beloved consort has received in your honour's house.

MASTER: My dear sir, you really must be soft in the head!

SOLDIER: All right, Mr Fancy Boots,[121] you'd better hand her over to me right now or you'll never enter your house again.

MASTER: What nonsense! Who's going to stop me?

SEXTON PASILLAS *returns, armed with the lid of a wine jar and a very rusty sword. He is accompanied by* SEXTON, GRAJALES, *carrying a helmet and a stick with a fox's brush attached to it.*[122]

SEXTON: Here you are, Grajales my friend, here's the man who's disturbing my peace of mind.

GRAJALES: I'm just sorry my weapons are so feeble and flimsy. Otherwise, I'd waste no time sending him to meet his Maker.

MASTER: Just a moment, gentlemen. What's this uproar and talk of violence?

SOLDIER: Thieves! So you've ganged up to betray me! What a

pair of fakes! I swear I'll puncture you full of holes, so don't try any of your monkey-tricks on me! Coward! Are you going to attack me with that feather duster? Do you take me for a drunkard, or a plaster statue that could do with a dusting?

GRAJALES: No, I'm just here to keep the flies away from a certain jar of wine.

CRISTINA *and her* MISTRESS *appear at the window.*

CRISTINA: Come quickly, madam, they're killing the master. There must be a couple of thousand of them – their flashing swords are quite blinding!

MISTRESS: God preserve him! You're quite right, my dear. May St Ursula and her virgins be his shield![123] Come Cristina, we must go down and do what we can to help him.

MASTER: Stop, gentlemen, for your own sakes! It's wrong to treat anyone with discourtesy!

SOLDIER: Keep back, you with that stinking duster; hold off, little lid bearer! Don't drive me into a rage, for if you do, I'll kill you and gobble you up and spew you out on the far side of hell.

MASTER: Stop, I say! If not, I swear to God I'll lose my temper and somebody will be sorry.

SOLDIER: I've put up my sword out of respect for you and the holy image you keep in your house.

SEXTON: Even if that image can work miracles, it won't save you this time.

SOLDIER: What impudence! Just try scaring me with a feather duster! Why, I've faced some of the most devastating cannon-fire you can imagine and never turned a hair.[124]

Enter CRISTINA *and her* MISTRESS.

MISTRESS: Dear husband, light of my life, you're not hurt are you, by any misfortune?

CRISTINA: Woe is me! I might have known my sexton and my soldier were at the bottom of this business.

SOLDIER: Now she treats me like the sexton: she called me 'her' soldier, too.

MASTER: I'm not hurt in the least, madam, but you should know that Cristinica is the cause of this squabble.

MISTRESS: How can Cristinica be the cause?

MASTER: From what I can understand, these gallant gentlemen are rivals for her favour.

MISTRESS: Is this true, girl?

CRISTINA: Yes, madam.

MISTRESS: Just listen to the shameless creature! Has either one of them abused you?

CRISTINA: Yes, madam.

MISTRESS: Which one?

CRISTINA: The sexton abused me on the way to the slaughterhouse.

MISTRESS: How often have I told you, sir, that this girl is not to leave the house! She's a big girl now and we shouldn't let her out of our sight. What will her father say? He handed her over to us so fresh and unspoiled. Where did he take you, slut, when he abused you?

CRISTINA: Nowhere in particular. It was in the middle of the street.

MISTRESS: What do you mean, in the middle of the street?

CRISTINA: Right there in the middle of Toledo Street, in the sight of God and everyone else, he called me dirty, immoral, shameless and without self-respect – and plenty more – all because he's jealous of that soldier over there.

MASTER: So there's been nothing more between you beyond the names he called you in the street?

CRISTINA: Of course not. After that he calmed down.

MISTRESS: Oh ... I can breathe again. That gave me a nasty turn!

CRISTINA: What's more, everything he said is written down in this document he gave me, promising to be my husband. I'm keeping it safe, wrapped in a cloth like a gold nugget.

MASTER: Give it to me, let's see it.

MISTRESS: Read it to us, husband.

MASTER: Here's what it says:

> I, Lorenzo Pasillas, under-sexton of this parish, swear that I truly – very truly – love Miss Cristina de Parrazes. To this effect, I do give her this document, signed with my name in the cemetery of St Andrew's parish in Madrid, on the 6th day of May, in this year of our Lord, 1611. Witnessed by: my heart, my intellect, my will and my memory.[125]Signed *Lorenzo Pasillas.*

What an unusual marriage contract!

SEXTON: When I say that I love her truly, I mean that I'm ready to do whatever she wants. To give one's heart is to give everything.

MASTER: So if she's agreeable you're prepared to marry her?

SEXTON: With the greatest of pleasure, even though I stand to lose a tidy sum that, from what I hear, my grandmother plans to settle on me when I take orders.

SOLDIER: If surrendering one's heart counts for anything around here, then I already surrendered mine to Cristina (together with all the other vital parts) when I crossed the Segovia Bridge more than a month ago.[126] If she cares to become my wife she can boast that her husband is custodian of a famous castle, instead of a sexton who isn't even a full one – just a half, and that half is probably lacking something.

MASTER: Would you like to get married, Cristinica?

CRISTINA: Yes I would.

MASTER: Then choose the one you like best of these two suitors.

CRISTINA: I'm too shy.

MISTRESS: You have no need to be. After all, choosing a mate is like choosing one's food: it's a matter of personal taste. No one else can make the choice for you.

CRISTINA: You and the master have brought me up and you'll pick me a suitable husband. Still, I would like a say in the matter.

SOLDIER: Young lady, just take a look at me. Note my fine figure. I'm a soldier and I intend to have my own castle. I'm brave-hearted and a most gallant gentleman. What's more, if you pull this thread of my clothing here you'll soon find out what kind of a gentleman I am underneath.[127]

SEXTON: Cristina, I'm a musician ... of bells. There isn't a sexton to touch me when it comes to arranging funerals or decorating the church for a solemn occasion. I can still carry out those duties when I'm married, so we'll eat like kings.

MASTER: Very well, my girl. Choose the one you like best and I'll accept your decision. That way you'll settle the quarrel between these mighty rivals.

SOLDIER: I'll submit to your choice.

SEXTON: I'll abide by it too.

CRISTINA: Then I choose the sexton.

MASTER: Call my neighbour the barber and ask him to send over his apprentices to lend their voices and their guitars to the wedding celebrations. I invite the soldier to be our guest.

SOLDIER: I gladly accept,
                For when the matter's signed and sealed,
                There's nothing left to be appealed.

Enter MUSICIANS

MUSICIANS: We came in at the right moment – that'll be our cue.

                For when the matter's signed and sealed,
                There's nothing left to be appealed.

SOLDIER: A woman's choice is always odd,
                Good taste is not her guide or rule,
                She never looks at worthy men,
                Prefers to trifle with a fool.
                A ragged soldier cannot match
                A sexton's higher bid for favour,
                For when it comes to love or cash,
                She'll choose the cash and never waver.
                Now some will think her choice is wise,
                Casting her lot as a sexton's bride,
                But many who run to the door of the church
                Find there are robbers and turncoats inside.

MUSICIANS: For when the matter's signed and sealed,
                There's nothing left to be appealed.

SEXTON: A soldier often makes rash claims
                When rich in years but poor in purse;
                In love there's company in two,
                The odd man out is just perverse.
                Pretending he's like a knight of old,
                Besieging the castle, rescuing the dame,
                While I prefer the quieter way
                Which, in the end, wins me the game.
                Your threats and insults leave me cold,
                For you have fought and lost the day,
                The loser at cards, in love and war,
                Curses his luck and cries 'Foul play!'

MUSICIANS: For when the matter's signed and sealed,
                There's nothing left to be appealed.

                [*They leave the stage, dancing and singing.*]

THE MAN WHO PRETENDED
TO BE FROM BISCAY

INTRODUCTION

A blend of traditional elements and contemporary references contributes to the elusive and intriguing quality of this Interlude. It recalls several familiar themes – the swindler who replaces a gold chain with a worthless replica; the deceiver who becomes the victim; the ridiculing of a prostitute; the stock portrayal of a Basque as a gullible fool – once again Cervantes takes the stereotypes and transforms them into his own creation.

The action is linked to a contemporary event, the promulgation in 1611 of a law known as the 'Premática de los coches'. This law was directed against a number of abuses considered to be wasteful and immoral, principally the practice of using coaches to further prostitution. Henceforth, only women of unquestionable social standing ('mujeres principales') were allowed to ride in coaches, provided they did not cover their faces with veils ('tapados'). As the Interlude makes clear, the object of this regulation was to prevent prostitutes from masquerading as ladies. Men were also prohibited from riding in coaches, no matter what their social standing (with the exception of doctors and the like, who were required to apply for a special licence). The reason for this directive was the perception that men were becoming soft and effeminate. The prostitute Cristina observes:

> From what I hear, the Spanish cavalry has been in a bad way ever since packs of young gentlemen have taken to squeezing into coaches and flogging around the streets at all hours of the day and night. They've quite forgotten the existence of horses and horsemanship.

This decline clearly undermines that most revered of many virtues – chivalry. Cristina echoes the reasoning of contemporary moralists when she concludes: 'So, if they have to do without the comfort of their galleys on wheels – I mean their coaches –

they'll go back to the chivalrous profession like their ancestors before them.'

The piece is an ironic commentary on the contemporary concern with the breakdown of traditional class barriers. The coach becomes a symbol of this breakdown, since it offers the opportunity for deception on the one hand and dereliction of duty on the other. At the same time Cervantes makes clear through the conversation between the two prostitutes that it is too late to put the clock back – the Spanish cavalry has already been supplanted by the infantry (a professional body recruited from all classes).[128] Cristina is quick to suggest that the prostitutes should profit from this example by turning the new law to their advantage:

CRISTINA: So, like the infantry, we girls can show ourselves off on foot with all our finery and charm. What's more, we no longer have to cover our faces. Since it's quite clear what's on offer, no one can complain that he's been deceived!

There is further irony: although the new law aims to uncover what has previously been veiled or hidden inside the coaches, this will not necessarily end the deception. The plot centres on a hoax involving two gold chains, one genuine, the other a counterfeit. Cristina's suspicions are dispelled by the assurances of her neighbour the silversmith. He, in turn, is convinced that the chain is the one he has seen before. Both are duped by appearances.

The theme of deception is extended into the title itself. We may wonder why the Interlude takes its name from the least prominent of the four main characters. Perhaps the reason is that, like the false chain, Quiñones is also not what he appears to be. What is more, by having Quiñones impersonate someone from the Basque country, Cervantes could count on a certain response from the public. The comic stereotype was expected to be simple and gullible, obstinate and tight-fisted, fond of wine and, above all, inarticulate.[129] The real Quiñones reveals himself to be none of these.

This Interlude further intrigues us by the way in which it starts '*in media res*' with Solorzano's reference to a previous encounter with the woman whom he plans to trick. (In fact, it is clear that he intends to get his own back for something she has previously done to him.)[130]

We are also aware of an underlying tension, not only between the sexes, but also between classes. Solorzano and Quiñones are idle young aristocrats. Like their counterparts in several of Cervantes's *Exemplary Novels* (for example, *Rinconete and Cortadillo*) they amuse themselves by consorting with the lower classes. Although Solorzano hastens to assure his companion that the trick he plans is harmless and will offend no one, we cannot help feeling that his social position gives him an unfair advantage over his victim.[131]

It has recently been suggested that the entire Interlude 'is circumscribed by a discourse that alludes to a degradation of concepts that originally concerned the sphere of noble life',[132] If this perception is valid, the satire goes to the roots of contemporary Spanish society and no one is spared in this corruscating piece. As Quiñones notes in the last line of the play, 'everything will come out clean in the wash' ('todo saldrá en la colada'). In the end everyone is unmasked.

CAST

SOLORZANO
QUIÑONES
CRISTINA
BRIGIDA
SILVERSMITH
SERVANT
CONSTABLE
TWO MUSICIANS

THE MAN WHO PRETENDED TO BE
FROM BISCAY

(El vizcaino fingido)

Enter SOLORZANO *and* QUIÑONES.

SOLORZANO: These are the two bags – to all appearances a
perfect match – and here are the chains to go inside them.
Now all I need is for you to fall in with my plan. In spite of
that woman's sharp wits (she's from Seville, you know), this
time she's going to fall right into the trap.

QUIÑONES: Why are you so anxious to deceive a woman? You
take it so seriously one would think your honour was at stake.

SOLORZANO: When women are like this one, it's a pleasure to
play tricks on them. Especially since the trick isn't going to
get out of hand: I mean it won't offend God or harm anyone.
A trick's no fun if it causes ill-feelings.

QUIÑONES: All right. If that's what you want, I'll go along with
it. I promise I'll help you with everything you mentioned and
I'll match you swindle for swindle. Does that satisfy you?
Where are you going now?

SOLORZANO: Straight to that strumpet's place. Meanwhile,
don't you stir from the house. I'll call you when it's time.

QUIÑONES: I'll be rooted to the spot and waiting for you.
[*They both exit. Enter Mistress* CRISTINA, *without her cloak
and Mistress* BRIGIDA, *who is flustered and alarmed.*]

CRISTINA: Lord, what's the matter with you, my dear Brigida?
You look as though you're about to give up the ghost.

BRIGIDA: Sweet friend, give me air, splash water on my face.
I'm dying. I'm done for. My soul is being wrenched from me.
God be with me! Let me make my confession without delay!

CRISTINA: What's this? Mercy me! Won't you tell me what has
happened to you? Have you seen an evil spirit? Did you
receive news that your mother was dead, or that your
husband's coming home? Has someone stolen your jewels?

BRIGIDA: I've seen no evil spirit, my mother's not dead, and my
husband's not coming home because his present business will

keep him another three months.[133] No one stole my jewels, either. Something much worse has happened.

CRISTINA: Come, Brigida, my sweet, tell me what it is. You've quite upset me and I'll be on tenterhooks until you tell me.

BRIGIDA: Well dearie, you'll be involved in this bad business too. Wipe my face: like the rest of my body, it's drenched in ice-cold sweat. What an unhappy lot we are, we women who lead such a free life! No sooner do we scrounge a bit of power than they clip our wings and take it away from us.

CRISTINA: Come to the point, dear friend, for pity's sake. Tell me what's happened to you. What's this misfortune that I'm going to be involved in?

BRIGIDA: Indeed you'll be involved in it! Quite a bit if you keep your wits about you – which you always do, of course. I tell you, dearie, on my way here I passed by the Guadalajara Gate.[134] A crowd of people and some officers of the peace were listening to a town crier while he proclaimed a ban on coaches and on women walking in the street with their faces covered.[135]

CRISTINA: Is that the bad news?

BRIGIDA: Well, what could be worse for us?

CRISTINA: I think it just means they're tightening up the law on the use of coaches. They couldn't possibly ban them completely! In fact, it might even be a good thing. From what I hear, the Spanish cavalry has been in a bad way ever since packs of young gentlemen have taken to squeezing into coaches and flogging around the streets at all hours of the day and night. They've quite forgotten the existence of horses and horsemanship. So, if they have to do without the comfort of their galleys on wheels – I mean their coaches – they'll go back to the chivalrous profession like their ancestors before them.[136]

BRIGIDA: Ah, Cristina, I also heard that some coaches are still permitted, but on condition that they're not lent out or used for . . . you know what![137]

CRISTINA: Let them do their worst! You must know, Brigida, that those who follow the fortunes of war can't agree on which is better, the cavalry or the infantry. They've finally decided that the Spanish infantry is the best in the world. So, like the infantry, we girls can show ourselves off on foot with all our finery and charm. What's more, we no longer have to cover our faces. Since it's quite clear what's on offer, no one can complain that he's been deceived!

BRIGIDA: Ah, Cristina, don't tell me that! How sweet it was to stretch out in the back of a coach, only revealing your face when you chose, and to someone who took your fancy. God rest my soul, I swear to you that every time I got my hands on a coach and took charge, I was so carried away I really thought I was someone important. I even fancied I was waited on by titled ladies!

CRISTINA: You see, Brigida, I'm right to say that we're better off without coaches, if only because it saves us from the sin of presumption. What's more, coaches made all women equal, whether or not they had something to offer, and that just wasn't fair. Why, if a stranger saw a woman in a coach with elegant clothes and glittering jewels he could easily forget himself and treat her like a noble lady. So, my friend, you mustn't be upset: you should make the most of your dashing manner and fine appearance; put on your best silk cloak and your new shoes – the ones with the silver trim on the heels – and turn yourself loose on the streets.[138] I assure you there'll be no shortage of flies if you let them taste the honey. Forbidden fruit is always the sweetest!

BRIGIDA: God bless you, dear, you've quite cheered me up with your comments and advice. What's more, I mean to act on them. I'll polish and preen myself. I'll put my best foot forward and kick up my heels.[139] No one's going to clip my wings, for the man everyone takes to be my husband is no such thing, although, mind you, he's promised to marry me.

CRISTINA: Good Lord. Is it possible that someone has entered my house without knocking? What do you want here, sir?

Enter SOLORZANO

SOLORZANO: Pardon the intrusion, madam. Opportunity makes thieves of us all. I found the door open and walked in; now I'm inside I make so bold as to offer you my services, not with words but with deeds. If I may speak in front of this lady, I'll explain what brings me here.

CRISTINA: Judging by your good appearance, sir, one may assume that your words and deeds are of the best. You may speak freely, for Mistress Brigida is such a close friend you could even call her my double.

SOLORZANO: With that assurance and your permission, I can

speak truthfully ... And it's the truth, madam, when I tell
you that I'm one of His Majesty's subjects whom you don't
yet know.[140]

CRISTINA: That's true enough.

SOLORZANO: For a long time I've wanted to offer you my
services in recognition of your beauty, your good nature, and
your admirable modesty. However, my ever-present difficult-
ies have prevented me until now: it's just my luck that a great
friend of mine in Biscay has sent me his son who's quite a
fellow for the women! He asks me to take him to Salamanca
and find him a tutor to instruct him and look after him.[141] To
tell you the truth, madam, the boy's rather obstinate and a bit
of an ass. What's more, he suffers from a defect that's hard to
talk about, and even worse to put up with: I mean he's rather
fond of ... shall we say ... sampling the wine. That doesn't
mean that he completely loses his wits, although he certainly
becomes fuddled, and when he's slightly tipsy, or even deep
in his cups, it's wonderful to see how merry and generous he
becomes. He bestows all his possessions on anyone who asks
for them, and even on those who don't. Since everything he
owns is going to the devil, I'd like to get my hands on some
small token. The best plan I could think of was to bring him
to your house, madam, because he's very fond of the ladies,
and we can fleece him on the quiet. For a start, madam, I'll
give you this bag: it contains a gold chain worth a hundred
and twenty ducats. Take it, madam, and give me ten ducats
right now so that I can buy a few trifles that I need. It'll cost
you another twenty ducats for dinner tonight for our ass, or
rather, our buffalo, since I'm leading him by the nose (as the
saying goes). In no time the chain will be yours alone, for I
want nothing more than the ten ducats I asked for just now.
It's a very fine chain, made of the best gold, an excellent piece
of workmanship. Here it is: take it, madam.

CRISTINA: I'm deeply grateful to you, sir, for thinking of me in
such a profitable connection. Yet, to be honest with you, I'm
quite confused by your generosity, perhaps even a bit
suspicious.

SOLORZANO: What are your suspicions, madam?

CRISTINA: That the chain is a fake. After all, they do say that
all that glitters is not gold.

SOLORZANO: You speak with exceptional wisdom, madam. It's

easy to see why they call you the wisest lady in Madrid. I'm delighted to see how plain and straightforward you are in confiding in me. Well, there's a remedy for everything except death. Just put on your cloak and go down to Silversmiths' Alley[142] (or else send someone you can trust): have them examine and weigh the chain. If the quality is as good as I've said, then you can give me the ten ducats, the young ass will have his treat and you'll get to keep the chain.

CRISTINA: Well, I know a silversmith who lives a stone's throw from here. He can easily set my mind at rest.

SOLORZANO: That's what I must truly desire and advise. God smiles on a straightforward transaction.

CRISTINA: If you'll just trust me with that chain, sir, while I satisfy myself, you can come back in a little while and I'll have ten gold ducats for you.

SOLORZANO: Excellent! Do you think I'd trust you with my honour and not with the chain? Have it tested several times over. I'm leaving now and I'll be back in half an hour.

CRISTINA: If my neighbour is at home you may come back sooner.

[*Exit* SOLORZANO]

BRIGIDA: Cristina, this is more than lucky – it's heaven-sent! Unhappy me, with my luck I never meet anyone who'll give me as much as a pitcher of water for nothing. Only a poor poet whom I met in the street was kind enough to give me a sonnet about the tragedy of Pyramus and Thisbe.[143] What's more, he offered me three hundred more in praise of myself.

CRISTINA: You'd have done better if you'd met a banker from Genoa who'd give you three hundred shillings.

BRIGIDA: Yes, indeed. However, those gentlemen are in no shape to come to your hand like falcons to a decoy. The new decree has left them quite dejected and out of sorts.[144]

CRISTINA: See here, Brigida, I want you to be clear about one thing: a Genoese banker who's gone broke is still worth more than four fully fledged poets! Why, everything's turning out for the best! Here comes my silversmith.

Enter the SILVERSMITH.

What do you want, good neighbour? I was just about to put on my cloak and go out to look for you.

SILVERSMITH: Mistress Cristina, I've come to beg you a favour: say that you'll do all you can to persuade my wife to go with you tomorrow to the theatre. I need – indeed, I have to be sure that I can spend tomorrow afternoon free from all interruption.

CRISTINA: I'll do it gladly. More than that, my friend, if you should need my house, it'll be empty and entirely at your disposal. I know what that kind of business can lead to.

SILVERSMITH: No madam, it will be enough if you can keep my wife occupied. Now, madam, what can I do for you, since you were looking for me?

CRISTINA: I just want you to weigh this chain for me and tell me how much it's worth.

SILVERSMITH: I've handled this chain many times, and I know that it weighs twenty-two carats for a value of a hundred and fifty gold ducats. If you want to buy it, madam, you'll have a good bargain, providing you don't have to pay a commission to the artist.

CRISTINA: Well, there's something to pay, but not much.

SILVERSMITH: Mind what you agree to, madam. Whenever you want to part with it, I'll charge you ten ducats for the commission.

CRISTINA: It'll cost me less, if I keep my wits about me. Now, neighbour, mind you aren't mistaken in estimating the quality and weight of the gold.

SILVERSMITH: Catch an expert like me making a mistake! I told you, madam, I've handled that chain several times, link by link. I've weighed it too. I know it as well as I know my own hands.

BRIGIDA: We'll be satisfied with that.

SILVERSMITH: As further proof, I know it has also been weighed and valued by a certain young gentleman of this city – Something de Solorzano is his name.

CRISTINA: That settles it. God be with you. I'll keep my side of the bargain. I'll take your wife to the theatre and keep her occupied for two hours afterwards, if necessary. After all, I know that an extra hour of entertainment can do no harm.

SILVERSMITH: They should bury us side by side in the same grave, madam! You know all my secrets! Farewell dear lady!

[*Exit the* SILVERSMITH]

BRIGIDA: Shouldn't we ask this Solorzano gentleman (for that must be his name) to find someone to help with my expenses when he brings along his friend from Biscay? He can even bring me a drunken Frenchman![145]

CRISTINA: You need not wait to ask him, for look, here he comes. There's purpose in his step. No doubt his ten ducats are spurring him on.

Enter SOLORZANO

SOLORZANO: Well, madam, have you completed your business? Is the chain vouched for?

CRISTINA: One last thing, sir, what's your name?

SOLORZANO: At home they call me Don Esteban de Solorzano. Why do you ask, madam?

CRISTINA: As final proof of your trustworthiness and integrity. Be good enough to wait here a moment with Mistress Brigida while I go and fetch the ten ducats.

[*She exits*]

BRIGIDA: Mr Solorzano, sir – would you by chance have a little trifle for me? To tell you the truth, I'm not to be sneezed at. What's more, my house has as many ways in and out of it as Mistress Cristina's. If I weren't afraid that someone would overhear us, I could tell you about several defects that she has: you should know that her breasts are like empty saddle-bags; her breath is bad because she puts too much paint on her face.[146] In spite of that, she's much sought after and in demand. I'm ready to scratch out my eyes, more from rage than envy, mind you, because men don't offer me their hand, although plenty give me the boot. Well, ugly women have all the luck . . .[147]

SOLORZANO: Don't lose heart, madam. If I have anything to do with it, there'll soon be another cock crowing in your roost.

CRISTINA *returns.*

CRISTINA: Here are the ten ducats, Mr Solorzano. The dinner tonight will be fit for a prince.

SOLORZANO: Our ass is waiting outside in the street, so I'll fetch him in. For my sake be kind to him, madam, even if he's hard to swallow.

[*Exit* SOLORZANO]

BRIGIDA: My dear, I asked him to bring someone to entertain me and he said that he would, by and by.

CRISTINA: By and by there'll be no one left to entertain us, my friend. There's much to be gained when one is young and much to lose when one is old.

BRIGIDA: I also told him how wealthy and pretty and charming you are – like a bouquet of ambergris, musk and civet wrapped in silk.

CRISTINA: My dear, I well know the compliments you pay people behind their backs!

BRIGIDA: (aside) To think that she has so many suitors! Why, the sole of my boot is worth more than the hoops round her neck![148] Once again I say, ugly women have all the luck ...

Enter QUIÑONES *and* SOLORZANO.

QUIÑONES: Biscay, hands kiss me, madam. Serve me.

SOLORZANO: The gentleman from Biscay says that he kisses your hands, madam, and is at your service.

BRIGIDA: Ah, what a pretty language! Of course, I can't understand it, but it sounds very pretty.

CRISTINA: I kiss the gentleman's hands, too, and more if he wishes.

QUIÑONES: Seem good, beautiful. Also night this we dine. Chain you keep, sleep never, enough I give it.

SOLORZANO: My friend says that he thinks you are good and beautiful, madam. He asks you to prepare the dinner and says the chain is yours without any further obligation.[149] He just wants to give it to you.

BRIGIDA: Did you ever see such generosity? What a stroke of luck – a real godsend!

SOLORZANO: If there are any preserves and a little sip of wine for my friend from Biscay, I know he'll return the favour with interest.

CRISTINA: Of course, there's plenty of both! I'll go and fetch some. You couldn't be better treated if you were Prester John of the Indies![150]

[*Exit* CRISTINA]

QUIÑONES: Lady that stays, as good as left.

BRIGIDA: What did he say, Mr Solorzano?

SOLORZANO: He said that the lady who remains here (he means you, madam) is as good as the one who went in.

BRIGIDA: How truthful the gentleman is! On that score he's no fool!

QUIÑONES: Fool the devil. Biscayan clever you want when to have him.

BRIGIDA: I understand him. He's saying that the devil is the fool and that Biscayans are clever when they want to be.

SOLORZANO: You've hit the nail on the head!

CRISTINA *returns with a* SERVANT, *carrying a box of preserved fruit, a carafe of wine, a knife and a napkin.*

CRISTINA: The gentleman can eat without fear for his stomach. Everything in this house is the quintessence of cleanliness.

QUIÑONES: Sweet with me, wine and water you call good. Saint you show me; this I drink and another too.

BRIGIDA: Lord, how charmingly the good gentleman speaks, even though I can't understand a word!

SOLORZANO: He says that with sweets one can drink wine as well as water; that this wine is vintage St Martin and he'll take another glass.[151]

CRISTINA: Let him take a hundred! As many as he can swallow.

SOLORZANO: Don't give him any more, it makes him ill. He's showing signs already. I've told Master Azcaray that he must never drink wine, but he pays no attention to me.

QUIÑONES: We're leaving, for wine that rises and falls tongue is gag and feet is shackles. Evening I return, madam; be God with you.

SOLORZANO: Listen to him! Now, wasn't I right?

CRISTINA: What did he say, Mr Solorzano?

SOLORZANO: He said that wine gags his mouth and shackles his feet; he'll return this evening, and may God be with you, ladies.

BRIGIDA: My word, just look how glazed his eyes are! He's quite tongue-tied! Lord, how he stumbles! He's really had a lot to drink! In all my life I've never seen anything so pitiful. Such a young man and so drunk!

SOLORZANO: He was already well on the way when we left the house. Mistress Cristina, while you prepare the dinner I'll take him home to sleep off the effects of the wine. We'll return early this evening.

CRISTINA: Everything will be in apple-pie order, don't you worry, gentlemen.

[*Exit the Biscayan and* SOLORZANO]

BRIGIDA: Dear Cristina, show me that chain and watch my envy grow! How pretty it is, it's so new and shiny – and how little it cost! Well, Cristina, I must say that you're being showered with goodies (though I'm sure I don't know why) and good fortune is knocking at your door, without even being invited. Indeed, you're as lucky as can be. But you certainly deserve it for your good nature, your wholesomeness and your well-known modesty. Those qualities are enough to bewitch the least susceptible of men. Not like me – I'm not worth a fig. Take your chain, dear. I feel like bursting into tears – not because I'm envious of you, but because I feel so sorry for myself.

SOLORZANO *returns.*

SOLORZANO: The most terrible thing has happened to us!

BRIGIDA: Something terrible? What is it, Mr Solorzano?

SOLORZANO: On our way home we met a servant with letters from the father of our Biscayan friend. It seems that he's on his death-bed and orders his son to leave immediately if he wants to see him before he dies. The servant brought him money for the journey, and doubtless he'll set off at once. Madam, I took ten ducats from him to give you. Here they are, together with the ten that you gave him earlier. Give me back the chain. If the father lives, his son will return it to you, or my name isn't Esteban de Solorzano.

CRISTINA: I'm truly sorry to hear the news, not on my own account, but for the sake of the unfortunate young man. I was becoming quite fond of him!

BRIGIDA: That's an easy way of earning ten ducats! Take them, dear, and hand the chain over to Mr Solorzano.

CRISTINA: Here you are. Give me the money. As a matter of fact, I expected to spend more than thirty ducats on the dinner. (*She gives him the chain.*)

SOLORZANO: Mistress Cristina, you can't fool an old dog; don't try to pull the wool over my eyes; pick on someone else to bamboozle . . .

CRISTINA: Why are you talking in riddles, Mr Solorzano?

SOLORZANO: To make you understand, madam, that your greed gives you away. Did you lose confidence in me so quickly, madam, that you cried wolf before there was any danger? Mistress Cristina, it's bad enough to lose honest earnings, but when they're ill-gotten it's downright dangerous. Give me my real chain and keep your fake one. Don't try any mythical metamorphoses on me,[152] especially in such a small space! Son-of-a-whore, what a clever bit of imitation! How swiftly executed!

CRISTINA: My dear sir, what are you saying? I don't understand you.

SOLORZANO: I'm saying that this is not the chain that I left with you, madam, although it looks the same. This is a forgery, while the other is made of twenty-two-carat gold.

BRIGIDA: I swear that's what our neighbour said, too, and he's a silversmith.

CRISTINA: This must be the devil's work!

SOLORZANO: Devil or no devil, produce my chain. That's enough shouting and swearing.

CRISTINA: The devil take me (or rather, may he not take me) if that isn't the chain that you left with me, sir. I've not laid hands on another. God knows, I can't be accused of that!

SOLORZANO: There's no reason to shout, especially as we have a magistrate whose job it is to protect everyone's rights.

CRISTINA: If this affair gets into the magistrate's hands, I'm done for. He takes such a poor view of me that he'll think I'm telling lies when it's the truth and he'll mistake my virtues for vices. Dear sir, if these hands have ever held another chain may they turn putrid and decay!

Enter a CONSTABLE.

CONSTABLE: What's all this shouting? Who's that cursing and crying?

SOLORZANO: Constable, you've come along in the nick of time. An hour ago I left a chain with this trollop from Seville as security against a loan of ten ducats. When I came back to claim my chain (which weighs twenty-two carats in gold and is worth a hundred and fifty gold ducats) she gave me this fake that isn't worth two ducats. Now she wants to make my complaint public by shouting it from the rooftops, even though she knows that this lady, who saw everything, will testify that what I say is true.

BRIGIDA: Indeed I saw everything happen – as large as life. As God is my witness, I swear this gentlemen is telling the truth. Yet I can't imagine where the switch was made: that chain has never left this room.

SOLORZANO: The constable can do me the favour of taking this lady to the magistrate and we'll all find out.

CRISTINA: I tell you again, if you take me before the magistrate, I'm a dead duck.

BRIGIDA: That's right, she's in his bad books.

CRISTINA: I'll hang myself right now; I'll commit suicide; the witches will have my blood.

SOLORZANO: Well now, Mistress Cristina, I'd like to do something for you, if only to deprive the witches of your blood; at the very least, to stop you from hanging yourself. This chain is very like the good one that belongs to the Biscayan. He's a fool and a bit of a drunkard. I'll take it to him and pretend it's his. So, madam, just make sure you show the constable your gratitude and pay for tonight's dinner. Then you can rest easy, for it's no great loss.

CRISTINA: May Heaven reward you, sir! The constable shall have six ducats and I'll spend one on the dinner. As for you, Mr Solorzano, I'm your slave for ever!

BRIGIDA: I'm going to dance until I drop!

CONSTABLE: Sir, you have shown yourself to be a fine, generous gentleman: one who knows how to serve the ladies.

SOLORZANO: Let me have the ten ducats I paid you in addition to what was owed.

CRISTINA: Here they are, as well as the six that I promised the constable.[153]

    Enter TWO MUSICIANS *and the Biscayan*, QUIÑONES

MUSICIANS: We've heard everything you've been saying and here we are!

QUIÑONES: Now I can tell Mistress Cristina that she swallowed the bait, hook, line and sinker!

BRIGIDA: Do you notice how clearly our Biscayan friend is speaking?

QUIÑONES: I only garble my words when it suits me.

CRISTINA: I'll be damned if those rascals haven't completely bamboozled me!

QUIÑONES: (*To the* MUSICIANS) Gentleman, do you remember that ballad I taught you? What are we waiting for?

MUSICIANS: When women think they know what's what
           They nothing know – or not a lot.
    The women who aspire to use
    Words affected and quite fancy,
    To cut a swath with rapier tongue
    And hold their own in lofty talk;

Or those who claim to know by heart
The plots of novels, good and bad:
To know which Phoebe loves which swain,
Or which true knights complete their quest;
Women who are fond of reading
Six times a month the strange exploits
Of Don Quixote and his squire.
    When women think they know what's what,
    They nothing know – or not a lot.
Those who trust to wits and cunning,
Full of wiles and snares and ruses,
Spurred by ambition or by greed,
To reach for power beyond their grasp;
Those who venture into water
Thinking it peaceful, safe and calm,
Before they find the hidden depths
That quickly draw them down inside;
Those who think themselves the winners,
The highest peak that tops the cream,
Conquering all with happy charm . . .
    When women think they know what's what,
    They nothing know – or not a lot.

CRISTINA: Very well, I confess I was taken in. Be that as it may, I invite you all to dine tonight.

QUIÑONES: We accept your invitation, and everything will come out clean in the wash![154]

THE MARVELLOUS
PUPPET SHOW

INTRODUCTION

The story of the Emperor's new clothes is familiar to modern readers in the version told by the nineteenth-century Danish storyteller Hans Christian Andersen. However, the origins of the story go back much further and can be found in written and oral versions throughout Europe. In Spain it appeared in the fourteenth century in *El Conde Lucanor*, a book of stories by the Infante Don Juan Manuel.[155]

In Cervantes's hands it becomes a teasing, enigmatic piece, artfully adapted to reflect his own views on contemporary Spain, and constantly challenging to modern critics. As Eugenio Asensio notes, none of Cervantes's Interludes 'is more deliberately ambiguous, or more open to conflicting interpretations'.[156]

As social satire it has much in common with *The Election of the Magistrates of Daganzo*. Both pieces portray the pretensions and prejudices of officials in rural communities. Once again, their prejudice is directed against Jews, although, according to Maurice Molho, it is unlikely that they would actually have known any Jews. Those who remained in Spain after 1492 as New Christians were traditionally associated with urban areas, where they worked in trade or as bankers, doctors or lawyers. No matter, the townspeople are fearful of being taken for Jews because this 'mistake' represents the negation of their own worthiness as Old Christians (i.e. the proof of 'untainted blood'). As Molho puts it: 'The man who declares "I am not a Jew" is expressing his fear of being one – referring to an obsessive and fantasised notion of Judaism, all the more laughable for being totally imaginary and unbelievable.'[157]

For these foolish townspeople, the fear of racial exposure is equalled by the fear of being proved illegitimate. In their eyes both conditions undermine the integrity of contemporary Spanish society. Molho sees this as satire aimed in particular at the wealthy peasant class, whose prosperity was becoming an influential factor in Philip III's Spain. They are ridiculed for aping aristocratic tastes (such as the luxury of celebrating a wedding by commissioning a private theatrical performance). While Cervantes invites his urban public to laugh at the pretensions of these country bumpkins, he also turns the mirror back to that public to remind them of their own irrational prejudices.[158]

Spadaccini and Talens interpret this Interlude as 'Cervantes's response to the myth of the integrated peasant ... propagated by the rural dramas of the period'.[159] That is to say, it ridicules the idealised portrayal of rustic life characteristic of the plays of Lope de Vega and his followers – the romantic view of the country as pastoral refuge from the Babylon of city life.[160]

The playful sliding between reality and illusion finds echoes in *Don Quixote* – particularly in the episode in which the knight watches a puppet show depicting the story of Melisendra and Don Gaiferos, mistakes it for real life and destroys the puppets (*Don Quixote* II, 26). There is, however, one important difference: in *The Marvellous Puppet Show* the audience has a strong incentive for accepting the illusion – the fear of being taken for social outcasts.

It can also be construed as a commentary on the nature of performance and its reception by an audience. The gullible audience is first conned into accepting the bogus performance by their expectation of what they will be shown, then forced to become accomplices to the hoax, not only because of their fear of exposure, but also because they have paid for the performance and are unwilling to admit that they have been robbed. Then, with typical sleight-of-hand, Cervantes turns the situation upside-down: the peasant audience not only accept the illusion, they take control of it with their own imagination (at one point the hoaxers are threatened by the Mayor – not because their deception has failed, but because it has succeeded too well!). Anarchy threatens until the intervention of the quartermaster and the soldiers restores a measure of order. As the unwitting de-mystifier, the quartermaster provides the means of closing the Interlude in a way that satisfies us, the external audience. For the *internal* audience (the peasants who have paid to see the puppet show) his arrival is providential, for it allows them to cast him as scapegoat. However, in another sense the matter is far from closed, since the peasants are still at loggerheads with the quartermaster, and the soldiers are about to arrive in the town. Instead of ending with the conventional song and dance, the Interlude remains open-ended: while the two hoaxers, bemused by their success, prepare to move on in search of further victims, the situation they have created is left to resolve itself off stage (as well as in the imagination of the external audience).[161]

It is tempting to see in this ambivalent closure a further reflection of Cervantes's views on contemporary theatre and audiences. From this perspective the Interlude creates an ironic fantasy in which an audience is manipulated into accepting an empty illusion – a view paralleled by Cervantes's many comments on the taste and intelligence of the average theatre-goer (the 'vulgo'). Conversely, it is also implied that audiences, however stupid, should not be underestimated: they can be unpredictable, even subversive, and in the end may succeed in hijacking the theatrical illusion. This anticipates the modern view that the way in which an audience reacts to performance is a highly subjective process and, consequently, not within the author's control. The fact that this view also runs counter to what Cervantes perceived to be the case with plays and audiences in his own time may further help to explain why he was so profoundly estranged from his contemporaries in the theatrical establishment.

CAST

CHANFALLA
CHIRINOS
RABELIN
GOVERNOR
BENITO REPOLLO
JUAN CASTRATO
PEDRO CAPACHO
JUANA CASTRATA
TERESA REPOLLA
BENITO'S NEPHEW
QUARTERMASTER
TOWNSPEOPLE

THE MARVELLOUS PUPPET SHOW

(El retablo de las maravillas)[162]

CHANFALLA: Don't forget what I told you, Chirinos, about this new hoax. I expect it to work as well as our trick with the rainmaker.[163]

CHIRINOS: Chanfalla, my noble friend, you can count on me to perform my part to perfection. My memory is the equal of my intellect, and both faculties are exceeded by my will to give you satisfaction. But tell me, why do we need this fellow Rabelin who's joined us? Aren't the two of us enough to carry off this trick?

CHANFALLA: He's as necessary to us as our daily bread: he'll play his lute to keep them occupied while they're waiting for the marvellous puppets to appear.

CHIRINOS: The real marvel will be if they don't stone him on sight! I've never seen such a miserable-looking creature in my life.

Enter RABELIN

RABELIN: Are we going to perform in this town, Mr Manager, sir? I can't wait to show your honour that by taking me on you've got yourself a good bargain.

CHIRINOS: If you were four times the size, the bargain would still be a poor one. We're done for unless your music amounts to more than you do.

RABELIN: We'll see about that. I want you to know that in spite of my size I've been invited to join a real acting company.[164]

CHANFALLA: If they give you the right part for your size you'll be almost invisible. Chirinos, we're almost inside the town. No doubt those people coming towards us are the Governor with the Mayor and Corporation. Let's go and meet them. Sharpen your tongue on the whetstone of flattery, but don't overdo it.

> *Enter the* GOVERNOR *with the Mayor,*
> BENITO REPOLLO, *Alderman* JUAN CASTRATO,
> *and the Notary,* PEDRO CAPACHO.

CHANFALLA: I kiss your worships' hands. Which one of your worships is the Governor of this town?

GOVERNOR: I am the Governor. What do you want, good fellow?

CHANFALLA: If I had two grains of sense, I would have realised that this perambulating and ample presence was none other than the distinguished Governor of this worthy town (may you never leave it for a better!).[165]

CHIRINOS: And certainly not during the lifetime of your wife and children – if your worship has a wife and children.

PEDRO: His worship the Governor is not married.

CHIRINOS: Well, whenever he does marry . . . There's no hurry.

GOVERNOR: So, what do you want, my honourable fellow?

CHIRINOS: Long live your worship for granting us this honour. Indeed, as the oak bestows acorns, the pear tree pears and the vine grapes, so a worthy man bestows honour, without so much as giving it a thought.[166]

BENITO: This is a saying worthy of Kickero.

PEDRO: His worship the Mayor surely means to say Cicero.

BENITO: I always mean to say whatever is best, but most of the time I make a botch of it. Anyway, fellow, what do you want?

CHANFALLA: Sirs, my name is Montiel and I bring with me the Marvellous Puppet Show. I've been summoned to Madrid to raise money for the hospitals with my performances. There's a scarcity of actor-managers just now and they're counting on me to save them from ruin.[167]

GOVERNOR: Why is it called the Marvellous Puppet Show?

CHANFALLA: It is called the Marvellous Puppet Show because of the marvellous things you can see and learn from it. It was devised and constructed by the magician Tomfool,[168] who used geometrical and astrological calculations, together with such signs, symbols and conjectures that whatever appears in the puppet show remains invisible to anyone who has the least drop of Jewish blood[169] in his veins, or was born out of wedlock. Those afflicted with either of these all too common complaints must just give up the idea of witnessing the wonders – never before seen or heard of – which my puppet show has to offer.

BENITO: Now I see that every day there is something new to be learned in this life! And you say the magician who invented this puppet show was called Tomfool?

CHIRINOS: His name was Tomfool; he was born in the city of Tomfootle and he was reputed to have a beard that reached down to his waist.

BENITO: For the most part men with long beards are very wise.

GOVERNOR: Mr Alderman Juan Castrato, with your persmission, I propose that your daughter Juana Castrata, my godchild, shall be married tonight. To liven up the celebration I should like Mr Montiel to set up his puppet show in your house.

JUAN: I shall be happy to obey your worship and to concur wholeheartedly with your wishes. Never mind the consequences.

CHIRINOS: One consequence is the little matter of payment. If we're not paid in advance you can forget about seeing our puppets. Most worthy gentlemen of the Law, you do have consciences and souls, don't you? It wouldn't do if people were to gatecrash the party tonight at Mr Juan Castrato's (or whatever his name is) and saw the show for nothing, so that tomorrow when we tried to charge the public to see it not a soul turned up. No, no, sirs: *ante omnia* you must pay us our just dues.

BENITO: Madam Manageress, no Antonia or Antonio[170] is going to pay you anything around here. Mr Alderman Juan Castrato will pay you more than handsomely, and if not, the Council will. You obviously don't know where you are. In this town, my good woman, we don't need any Antonia to pay up for us.

PEDRO: Upon my soul, Benito Repollo, you're way off the mark! The lady didn't mention any Antonia – she just asked to be paid in advance: before all else, that's what *ante omnia* means.

BENITO: Look here, Mr Notary Capacho: if people speak to me straight I can understand perfectly well. You are educated and well read, so you can understand this foreign gibberish, but I can't.

JUAN: Very well. Will the manager be satisfied with an advance of a half-dozen ducats ... as well as the assurance that no one from the town will be admitted to my house tonight?

CHANFALLA: Done! I trust your honour to keep your word.

JUAN: Come with me, then. I'll give you the money and you'll see how suitable my house is for setting up your puppet show.

CHANFALLA: Let's be off. But don't forget the conditions that must be met by everyone who wants to see the marvellous puppet show.

BENITO: I'll take care of that. As for me, I feel quite safe in submitting to the test. I'm sure of my pedigree: on all sides of my family I can boast whole barrelfuls of vintage Christian blood. I'll have no problem seeing the puppet show!

PEDRO: We all expect to see it, Mr Benito Repollo.

JUAN: None of us here was born in the sticks.

GOVERNOR: As far as I can see you'll really need to prove it, dear colleagues.

JUAN: Come along, Mr Manager. To business! My name is Juan Castrato, son of Anton Castrato and Juana Macha – I need say no more, so sure am I of being able to stand on my two feet and look the aforementioned puppet show full in the face.

CHIRINOS: God willing!

[*Exit* JUAN *and* CHANFALLA]

GOVERNOR: Tell me, madam, which poets are in fashion now in Madrid? Which ones have a reputation and a following? What about the playwrights? I pride myself on being a bit of a poet myself, and I have quite a weakness for the greasepaint too. In fact, I've just dashed off twenty-two new plays, and I'm waiting for the opportunity to take them to Madrid, where they are bound to make the fortune of several actor-managers.

CHIRINOS: Your worship, I don't know how to answer your question about the poets: there are so many of them that they blot out the sun and they all think they're the cat's whiskers. As for the playwrights,[171] the same old names are still around – they're not worth mentioning. But tell me, your worship, what name do you go by as a poet?

GOVERNOR: Madam, they call me Gomecillos, B.A.

CHIRINOS: God bless my soul, don't tell me you are *the* Gomecillos, B.A.! The author of those famous poems, 'Lucifer was feeling ill' and 'He suddenly throws up'![172]

GOVERNOR: Gossiping tongues have tried to saddle me with the parentage of those poems, but I'm no more responsible than the Great Turk.[173] The ones I did write and won't repudiate, are about the floods in Seville.[174] Although poets are notorious for stealing from each other I pride myself on stealing nothing from anyone. As long as God gives me a hand with my verses, I'll leave stealing to the others.

Enter CHANFALLA.

CHANFALLA: Will your worship be pleased to come inside? Everything is ready and we can begin.

CHIRINOS: *(aside)* Is the money in the bag?

CHANFALLA: *(aside)* Right next to my heart.

CHIRINOS: Imagine, Chanfalla – the Governor is a poet.

CHANFALLA: A poet! God's blood! Well then, he'll be easy to fool, because they're all simpletons, that lot: they're easy-going, gullible, and not given to suspicion.

BENITO: Come on, Mr Manager! I'm itching to see that box of wonders!

[*All exit*]

Enter two young country girls, JUANA CASTRATA *and* TERESA REPOLLA. JUANA *is dressed as a bride.*

JUANA: Come and sit here, Teresa dear, so that we're right in front of the stage. You know the conditions for seeing the show, so pay careful attention: it would be a great shame to miss it.

TERESA: Why, Juana, I'm your cousin – you know that. I wish I could be as sure of going to Heaven as I am of seeing whatever the show has to offer. Upon my mother's life, you can pluck the eyes from my face if I don't! A fine thing that would be for me!

JUANA: Keep still, cousin. Here they come.

Enter all the previous characters, together with other TOWNSPEOPLE *and* BENITO'S NEPHEW.

CHANFALLA: Take your seats everyone. Take note that the puppet theatre is placed behind this tapestry, and the manageress as well.[175] That's the musician over there.

BENITO: You call him a musician? Put him behind the tapestry too; though I could put up with the sight of him as long as I didn't have to listen to him!

CHANFALLA: You are quite mistaken, Mr Mayor, to take a dislike to the musician; believe me, he's a good Christian and a gentleman of sound breeding.

GOVERNOR: And one needs such qualities to be a good musician.

BENITO: Though his breeding may be sound, his sounds are pretty coarse.

RABELIN: That's all a poor devil gets for playing for the benefit of . . .

BENITO: Well, for God's sake, we've had other musicians here who were as . . .

GOVERNOR: Let's leave it at that, or you two gentlemen will never be done. I call on Mr Montiel to begin the show.

BENITO: This manager has very little baggage for such a big show.

JUAN: Everything must be worked by magic.

CHANFALLA: Your attention, ladies and gentlemen. We are about to begin. (*He strikes a pose and declaims*) O thou, whoever thou art, who built this theatre with such wonderful artifice that it has earned the reputation of being marvellous: through the power which it possesses, I entreat, beseech and command thee to demonstrate forthwith some of thy marvellous marvels to these assembled ladies and gentlemen, so that they may enjoy them and rejoice without fear of harm or offence. Ah, I see that thou hast granted my request, for over there I perceive the figure of Samson the brave embracing the pillars of the Temple, which he means to hurl to the ground so as to wreak vengeance on his enemies. Stop, valiant knight, stop, for God's sake! Don't commit such an outrage! We can't have you pulling it all down and flattening the distinguished group of gentry gathered here tonight.

BENITO: Spare me, you brute! A fine thing that would be! We come here to enjoy ourselves and end up as pancakes! Spare me, Sir Samson, in spite of my sins. Heed the prayers of these honest folk!

PEDRO: Do you see him, Castrato?

JUAN: See him? Why wouldn't I see him? Are my eyes in the back of my head?

GOVERNOR: (*aside*)This is an amazing business. I can no more see Samson than I can see the Great Turk. Yet there's no doubt that I'm legitimate and a true Christian.

CHIRINOS: Watch out, sir, here comes the very same bull that killed that poor wretch in Salamanca![176] Get out of the way, mister! Get out of the way! God save you! God save you!

CHANFALLA: Out of the way everybody, out of the way! Here toro, toro, toro!

(*They all move about in an uproar.*)

BENITO: That bull has the devil in him. He has a fierce and horny look. I'd better take care or he might toss me.

JUAN: Mr Manager, if you can, spare us the puppets that cause alarm. I don't ask it for myself, but for these young girls. That ferocious bull has turned them as white as sheets.

JUANA: No doubt of that, Father. It'll take me three days to get over it. I could just see myself on those horns . . . they look as sharp as a cobbler's awl.

JUAN: You wouldn't be my daughter if you couldn't see it.

GOVERNOR: (aside) That's done it. Everyone sees it but me; I'll have to say that I see it too, for the sake of my damned honour.

CHIRINOS: Those mice running about over there are the direct descendants of the mice who were raised on Noah's ark. Some of them are white, some are piebald, some speckled and some blue – in a word they're all mice.

JUANA: Jesus! Help me! Hold me fast or I'll throw myself out of the window. Mice! Oh woe is me! Cousin, pull your skirts tight about your legs and take care they don't bite! My, there are a lot of them! By my grandmother's white hair, there must be more than a thousand!

TERESA: I'm the one who should complain – they're climbing all over me. A little brown mouse has me fast by the knee. May Heaven help me, since no one here will.

BENITO: It's just as well I'm wearing breeches. No mouse can get at me, no matter how small.

CHANFALLA: This drenching rain that's pouring down on us comes from the source of the River Jordan. If it touches a woman's face her complexion will turn to burnished silver, and men will find themselves with beards of gold.[177]

JUANA: Cousin, do you hear that? Hold up your face; you could do with a spot of that. Oh, what a delicious taste! Cover up, Father, don't *you* get wet.

JUAN: We're all taking cover, Daughter.

BENITO: The water is running right down my back and out between my buttocks![178]

PEDRO: I'm as dry as a stick.

GOVERNOR: (aside) What the devil is this? Not a single drop has touched me although the others are drenched. What if I'm the only bastard here?

BENITO: Get rid of that musician, I say. If you don't, I swear to

God I'm leaving without waiting to see another puppet. The devil take that damned musician. There he goes, plucking away, but there's no instrument, nor any sound either.

RABELIN: Don't pick on me, Mr Mayor. I'm playing just as God has been pleased to instruct me.

BENITO: How could God be pleased to instruct you, you maggot? Get behind that blanket. If not, by God, I'll throw this bench at you.

RABELIN: I think the devil brought me to this town.

PEDRO: How fresh is the water from the blessed River Jordan! I covered myself as best I could, but a little bit still got on my moustache and I'll swear it has turned as fair as gold.

BENITO: Fifty times worse, I'd say.

CHIRINOS: Here come a bunch of rampant lions and honey bears. Take care all of you! They may look like fantastical beasts, but with their bared fangs they can still cause trouble and perform Herculean feats!

JUAN: God's teeth, Mr Manager, do you mean to fill the place with bears and lions?

BENITO: Just see how that Tomfool sends us lions and dragons instead of larks and nightingales! Mr Manager, either bring out puppets that are less alarming or we'll settle for what we've already seen and, as God is your guide, don't bother to stay in this town a moment longer.

JUANA: Mr Benito Repollo, for the sake of us ladies, let the bears and lions come out. We'll be well pleased if they do.

JUAN: But Daughter, how is it that just now you were scared of mice and now you are begging for bears and lions?

JUANA: Anything new gives pleasure, Father.

CHIRINOS: That young lady entering now, so attractive and elegant, that's Herodias.[179] She's the one whose dancing cost John the Baptist his head. If someone will help her dance, you'll really see something.

BENITO: God's truth! That's more like it! That puppet is a beauty – a real dazzler! Son-of-a-whore, how the wench wriggles! Nephew Repollo, you know how to play the castanets: lend her a hand and this will be quite a party!

NEPHEW: I'll be glad to, Uncle Benito.

(*A Saraband is played.*)

PEDRO: By my grandfather's whiskers! The Saraband and the Chaconne are old hat![180]

BENITO: Hey, Nephew, mind you keep up with that Jewish hussy! But if she's Jewish, how can she see the show?

CHANFALLA: Every rule has its exception, Mr Mayor.

A trumpet sounds off stage. Enter a QUARTERMASTER.[181]

QUARTERMASTER: Which of you is his worship the Governor?

GOVERNOR: I'm the Governor. What do you want, sir?

QUARTERMASTER: You are to find quarters right away for thirty cavalrymen. They'll be here in half an hour; sooner than that, in fact. I can hear the trumpet now, so I'll be off.

[*Exits*]

BENITO: I'll swear they've been sent by the magician Tomfool.

CHANFALLA: No such thing. It's just a company of cavalry that has been camping two leagues from here.

BENITO: Now I can see through this Tomfool; you and he are a pair of whopping rogues – I know you are – and that goes for the musician too! Listen to me, I'm ordering you to tell Tomfool that he'd better not dare send those cavalrymen or I'll have him horsewhipped: two hundred lashes on his back without a break.

CHANFALLA: I assure you Mr Mayor, Tomfool has nothing to do with the cavalrymen!

BENITO: I say that Tomfool is responsible for this, just as he's responsible for the rest of the hocus pocus I've seen here today.

PEDRO: We've all seen it, Mr Repollo.

BENITO: I'm not suggesting you haven't seen it, Pedro Capacho. (*to* RABELIN) Stop playing that music, you living nightmare, or I'll box your ears!

The QUARTERMASTER *returns.*

QUARTERMASTER: Well, are the billets ready? The cavalry are already in the town.

BENITO: So Tomfool is getting away with it, is he? Well, I promise you, manager of tricks and apparitions, that you will answer to me for this!

CHANFALLA: Take note, all of you, that the Mayor is threatening me.

CHIRINOS: Take note that the Mayor insists that the magician Tomfool is responsible for sending His Majesty's cavalry.

BENITO: God Almighty, I'll see you tomfooled too!

GOVERNOR: For my part I don't believe these cavalrymen can be a hoax.

QUARTERMASTER: A hoax, your worship? Are you in your right mind?

JUAN: They might well be tomfooleries – like the other things we've seen here. Mr Manager, bring out the young lady Herodias again so that this gentleman can see something exceptional. *(aside)* Perhaps we can use her as a bribe to get him to leave quickly.

CHANFALLA: Gladly ... See where she comes now, beckoning to her partner to dance with her again.

NEPHEW: She can count on me: I won't let her down.

BENITO: That's the way, Nephew. Keep her moving, keep her moving: round and round again! God's life, that girl's like quicksilver! Go to it, go to it! Again and again!

QUARTERMASTER: Are these people mad? What the devil do you mean by 'young lady'? What dance? Who is this Tomfool?

PEDROL: What? Do you mean to say, Mr Quartermaster, that you don't see Herod's girl over there?

QUARTERMASTER: The devil take me if I see any girl over there!

PEDRO: That does it! He's one of them![182]

GOVERNOR: He's one of them. He's one of them!

JUAN: He's one of them! The quartermaster is one of them. He's one of them!

QUARTERMASTER: I'm as much a whoreson as any one of you. By the living God, if I draw my sword you'll all leave by the window instead of the door!

PEDRO: I knew it! He's one of them!

BENITO: Right! He's one of them. He sees nothing!

QUARTERMASTER: You contemptible scum! If you say I'm one of them once more, I'll break every bone in your bodies.

BENITO: Jews and bastards always have been cowards: that's why we'll keep on saying 'he's one of them, he's one of them'.

QUARTERMASTER: To hell with these peasants. Just you wait!
    (He draws his sword and sets on them: MAYOR BENITO
    gives poor RABELIN *a beating while* CHIRINOS *takes
    down the blanket.)*

CHIRINOS: The arrival of the cavalry was the work of the devil. You'd think he'd summoned them with a trumpet!

CHANFALLA: What an extraordinary business this has been!

The reputation of the marvellous puppet show remains unchanged; tomorrow we can show it to the town, and we ourselves can claim victory in this battle. Long live Chirinos and Chanfalla!

THE MAGIC CAVE OF
SALAMANCA

INTRODUCTION

The magical properties of a cave in Salamanca became famous in a legend dating from the Middle Ages.[183] Nevertheless, the allusion to this well-known piece of folklore in the title of Cervantes's Interlude is somewhat tangential. Its relevance, in fact, relies on the audience's recognition of the implied subtext. The student, Carraolano, claims to have studied his 'art' ('ciencia') in the Cave of Salamanca. The gullible husband, Pancracio, immediately takes this to mean that the student has studied magic, and his curiosity is aroused. Just as the credulous townspeople in *The Marvellous Puppet Show* accept the trick that is played on them, so Pancracio's willingness to believe in magic makes a dupe of him.

The play also interweaves several stock comic themes and characters. The cuckolded husband deceived by his wife with the assistance of the maid; the sexton who appears as a lover or suitor; the student who dabbles in picaresque deceptions: these occur in other Interludes by Cervantes, as well as elsewhere in his writings.[184] They are also reminiscent of Lope de Rueda and other familiar sources.

Once again the piece seems fresh and original because it succeeds in fusing familiar elements into a satisfying whole. Although the participants are recognisable types, they are also clearly differentiated as individuals. The leading protagonist is undoubtedly Carraolano who outwits everyone and effectively stage-manages the final succession of events to his own advantage. In this, of course, he resembles the tricksters in *The Marvellous Puppet Show*, although, unlike them, he remains in control of events throughout.

CAST

PANCRACIO
LEONARDA
CRISTINA
STUDENT
SEXTON
BARBER
LEONISO

THE MAGIC CAVE OF SALAMANCA

(La cueva de Salamanca)

Enter PANCRACIO, LEONARDA *and* CRISTINA

PANCRACIO: Come madam, dry those tears and cease your sighing. After all, four days are not a lifetime! God willing, I'll not be away more than five days at the very most. All the same, to set your mind at rest, perhaps I should break my word and forget about this journey. My sister can get married without me.

LEONARDA: No, Pancracio, my lord and master, you must not give offence on my account. Go and do what is clearly your duty. I'll manage to bear my grief and endure my solitude as best I can. I only beg you to return as soon as possible, but not a day later. Let me lean on you, Cristina, for my heart fails me!

(LEONARDA *faints*.)

CRISTINA: Such a fuss about getting married! To put it plainly, master, if I were you I wouldn't stir from home.

PANCRACIO: Go in, girl, fetch some water and splash it in her face. But wait, I know some magic words to whisper in her ear: they're bound to revive her.

(*He whispers in* LEONARDA's *ear and she revives*.)

LEONARDA: Enough. It cannot be helped. We must resign ourselves, my love. The longer you delay here, the longer you deprive me of the pleasure of your return. Your friend Leoniso must be waiting for you in the carriage. May God go with you and bring you back to me quickly and without harm.

PANCRACIO: My angel, if you want me to stay I'll not leave your side.

LEONARDA: Oh no, no, joy of my life. Your wish is my command. Now you really must go, for what touches your honour touches mine as well.

CRISTINA: What an exemplary couple! If every wife loved her

husband as much as my mistress Leonarda loves hers, then life would be very different.

LEONARDA: Cristinica, bring me my cloak. I want to see your master off in the carriage.

PANCRACIO: No, my love. For my sake, embrace me now and stay here. Cristinica, take care of your mistress. When I return I promise you shall have a new pair of shoes.

CRISTINA: Be off, sir, and have no concern for your mistress. I mean to distract her so that she'll not dwell on your absence.

LEONARDA: Not dwell on his absence! What are you thinking of, girl?

When you are from me there's no joy or delight.
Sorrow and sadness are mine day and night.[185]

PANCRACIO: I can bear it no longer. Peace be with you, light of my eyes: they will look on nothing with pleasure until I return to your presence.

[*Exit* PANCRACIO]

LEONARDA: A pox on you! Begone and good riddance! This time your swaggering and your suspicions will get you nowhere!

CRISTINA: I was terrified your protestations would delay his departure and our pleasure.

LEONARDA: The guests we invited – are they coming tonight?

CRISTINA: But of course! I've already sent them word. They're so excited that this afternoon they sent round a hamper with the laundress who's in on our secret. Instead of linen, they filled it full of gifts and good things to eat – just like the treats the king hands out to the poor on Maundy Thursday – only this is more like an Easter hamper, with pies, chicken breasts and cold cuts, as well as puddings, two capons not yet plucked, and all kinds of fruit.[186] Best of all, there's a gallon of excellent wine that really tickles your nose.

LEONARDA: He's always thoughtful, my Reponce. My own sexton, who warms the cockles of my heart!

CRISTINA: What about Master Nicholas the barber, who thrills me through and through? Every time I see him, he shears away my cares as if they had never existed.

LEONARDA: Did you put the basket in a safe place?

CRISTINA: I've put it in the kitchen, hidden under a cloth.

The student, CARRAOLANO, *knocks at the door, then enters without waiting for an answer.*

LEONARDA: Cristina, see who that is at the door.

STUDENT: I'm just a poor student, ladies.

CRISTINA: I can tell by your clothes that you're a student and by your boldness that you're poor.[187] It's a strange thing: the poor never wait at the door for alms. They march right in and walk all over the house. They'll even wake up the household.

STUDENT: I expected a kinder reply from a lady such as you. After all, I'm not asking for alms. I'm just looking for a stable or a hayloft where I can shelter tonight from the foul weather.

LEONARDA: Where are you from, my friend?

STUDENT: I'm a Salamantine, my lady – that's to say, I'm from Salamanca. I was on my way to Rome with an uncle of mine, who died on the road in France. I found myself on my own and decided to return home. In Catalonia I was robbed by the servants, or henchmen, of the bandit Roque Guinart ... though if Roque had been there himself he would never have let them harm me: he's so polite and considerate – not to say charitable.[188] Nightfall overtook me just as I was passing your hospitable doors – for such I take them to be – and I hereby throw myself on your mercy.

LEONARDA: Indeed, Cristina, he has already moved me to pity.

CRISTINA: He breaks my heart. Let's keep him here tonight, for there's enough food to feed the king's army. I mean, he'll think the scraps alone are manna from Heaven.[189] What's more, he can help me pluck those birds.

LEONARDA: But Cristina, do we really want a witness to our peccadilloes?

CRISTINA: This one looks as though he can keep his mouth shut. Come here, my friend. What do you know about plucking?

STUDENT: What do I know about plucking? I don't know what you mean, good madam, unless you're referring to the state of my purse, in which case I freely admit that no one is more plucked than I am.[190]

CRISTINA: No, that's not what I mean at all. I simply want to know if you are capable of plucking a couple of capons.

STUDENT: Ladies, all I can say is that, by God's grace, I have my Bachelor's degree from Salamanca, and I won't say ...

LEONARDA: In that case, no doubt you are capable of plucking not just capons, but all manner of birds. Are you any good at keeping secrets, or are you, perhaps, given to revealing everything you see, feel or imagine?

STUDENT: I could be a witness to a massacre and never open my mouth.

CRISTINA: Well then, put a seal on your lips, sew up your tongue and sharpen your appetite. Come inside with us. You'll see something extraordinary and eat a magnificent dinner. Then you can take your pick of places to sleep in the hayloft.

STUDENT: That will suit me to perfection, for I'm neither greedy nor hard to please.

Enter the SEXTON *and the* BARBER.

SEXTON: Ah, at last, here are the celestial drivers who guide the chariots of our desires![191] They are the light of our darkness, the obliging foundations and pillars of our palace of pleasure!

LEONARDA: That's the only thing that irks me about him. Reponce, my love, for God's sake do use plainer language so that I can understand you. Don't climb to such dizzy heights where I can't follow you.

BARBER: One good thing can be said for me: my speech is as plain as the nose on my face. I call a shovel a spade and a spade a shovel, as the saying goes.

SEXTON: Yes, there has to be some difference between a sexton who knows his Latin and a barber brought up in the vulgar tongue.

CRISTINA: For my purposes the barber knows as much Latin as the famous grammarian Antonio Nebrija – perhaps even more![192] But that's enough talk about knowledge and fancy talk. We all speak as well as we can, even if it's not always correct. Now let's go in and get to work, for we have plenty to do.

STUDENT: And plenty of plucking . . .

SEXTON: Who is that fellow?

LEONARDA: A poor student from Salamanca who needs shelter for the night.

SEXTON: I'll give him a couple of coins for his dinner and lodging, and may God go with him.

STUDENT: Master Reponce, I'm grateful for your kind charity, but my lips are sealed; besides, I'm to do the plucking – to satisfy this good lady (for she's the one who asked me). I swear by . . . that I shan't leave this house tonight, no matter who gives the order. You have no choice, sir, but to trust a man of my quality who is willing to sleep in the hayloft ... and if you're afraid for your capons, may the devil pluck them and you can choke on them after you've eaten them.

BARBER: This fellow isn't just poor, he's a scoundrel as well! I'll wager he'll make off with everything, lock, stock and barrel!

CRISTINA: Upon my life, what fine sport this is! Let's all go in and see to what has to be done. The student can pluck and keep his mouth shut just as if he were at Mass.

STUDENT: Or better still, at Vespers.[193]

SEXTON: I don't trust this poor student. I swear he knows more Latin than I do.

LEONARDA: That must be why he has such sharp wits! But don't be ashamed of a charitable act, my friend, for, as the Bible says, 'charity never faileth'.[194]

[*They all leave. Enter* PANCRACIO *and his friend,* LEONISO.]

LEONISO: I knew that wheel was about to fall off. I never met a coachman who wasn't stubborn! If he had pulled over to avoid the ditch we'd be two leagues further on our way.

PANCRACIO: It's of no concern to me. I would prefer to spend the night at home with my wife Leonarda instead of at the inn. This afternoon when I left her she was ready to die at the thought of my leaving.

LEONISO: What a woman! Heaven has blessed you, my dear friend. You should be thankful.

PANCRACIO: I am indeed. I shall never be thankful enough. There's not another woman like her, so you may keep your Lucretias and your Portias.[195] She's a paragon of virtue and modesty.

LEONISO: If only my wife were not so jealous I would have no cause for complaint. My house is close by. If you take this street you'll come to yours. Let's meet again tomorrow. I'll see to it that we have another carriage then. Farewell.

PANCRACIO: Farewell.

[*They both leave.*]

The SEXTON *and the* BARBER *enter, carrying guitars. The* SEXTON *has his cassock tucked up and tied in at the waist. He dances as he plays the guitar, reciting while he cavorts.*

SEXTON: Fair is the night, fair the occasion, fair is the dinner and fair my love!

CRISTINA: Master Reponce, this is no time for dancing! First we'll see to dinner and the other business. The dancing can wait until afterwards.

SEXTON: Fair is the night, fair the occasion, fair is the dinner and fair my love!

LEONARDA: Let him be, Cristina. I dearly love to see his capers.
              (PANCRACIO *knocks at the door.*)

PANCRACIO: Ho there! Are you all asleep? Why is the door bolted so early? How careful my Leonarda is!

LEONARDA: What a disaster! That voice! It's my husband at the door. Something must have happened to bring him home. Gentlemen, you must hide in the coal-house – I mean in the loft – where we keep the charcoal.[196] Hurry Cristina, show them the way. I'll keep Pancracio occupied so as to give you time to hide them.

STUDENT: Foul is the night, sour the occasion, the dinner turns putrid and love rots away!

CRISTINA: A nice mess, I must say! Come this way, all of you.

PANCRACIO: (*off stage*) What the devil is going on? Why don't you open up, you sleepyheads?

STUDENT: This is where I make myself scarce. I'm not taking my chances with these gentlemen. Let them hide where they choose. Just take me to the hayloft: if I'm found there I'll be taken for a beggar, not an adulterer.

CRISTINA: Hurry up, or he'll bring the door down!

SEXTON: My heart is in my mouth.

BARBER: And mine in my heels!
              [*They all leave except for* LEONARDA, *who leans out of the window.*]

LEONARDA: Who's there? Who's that knocking?

PANCRACIO: Your husband, Leonarda my dear. Open up. I've been hammering on this door for half an hour.

LEONARDA: That seems to be the voice of my beloved jailer, but I cannot be sure, for one cock crows just like another.

PANCRACIO: What admirable caution! What a prudent woman. It is I, my love – your husband Pancracio. You can safely open the door.

LEONARDA: Come closer and I'll see about that. Tell me how I acted this afternoon when my husband left.

PANCRACIO: You sighed and you cried and then you fainted.

LEONARDA: That's true enough. But all the same, describe the birthmarks I have on one of my shoulders.

PANCRACIO: On your left shoulder you have a mole the size of a half ducat, with three hairs like the finest threads of gold.

LEONARDA: True again. And what's the name of the maid servant?

PANCRACIO: Come now, don't be so tiresome. Cristinica is her name. What more do you want?

LEONARDA: Cristinica, Cristinica: it's your master. Go down and open the door, girl!

CRISTINA: I'm going, madam. Thank God he's come safely home! What brings you back so soon, dear master?

LEONARDA: O my love! Tell us quickly what has happened. I'm quite faint with fear.

PANCRACIO: It was nothing serious. The carriage wheel came off in a ditch, so my friend and I decided to come home instead of spending the night in the country. Tomorrow we shall look for another carriage; we have plenty of time. But . . . who is that shouting?

Off stage, as if from far off, the STUDENT's *voice is heard.*

STUDENT: Open up! I'm suffocating!

PANCRACIO: Is he in the house or out in the street?

CRISTINA: I'll be hanged if it isn't the poor student I locked in the hayloft for the night!

PANCRACIO: A student locked up in my house and in my absence? Can I believe my ears? Truly, madam, if I were not so sure of your virtue, I would be somewhat suspicious. Go and let him out, Cristina. The hay must have fallen on him.

CRISTINA: I'm going.

[CRISTINA *exits*]

LEONARDA: My dear, it's just a poor student from Salamanca who begged us in God's name to give him shelter for the night – even if it was just the hayloft. You know how I am: I can't refuse anyone anything, so we locked him in. But here he comes. Look what a state he's in.

Enter the STUDENT *with* CRISTINA: *his beard, hair and clothes are covered in hay.*

STUDENT: If I were not so frightened and had less of a conscience, I'd have spared myself the risk of suffocating in the hayloft. I could have dined better, too, and had a softer bed.

PANCRACIO: Who, my friend, would have given you a better dinner and a softer bed?

STUDENT: Who? My art, of course ... If only my hands were not tied by my fear of the law.

PANCRACIO: Yours must be a dangerous art if you're afraid of the law!

STUDENT: If respect for the Holy Inquisition didn't prevent me from practising the art that I learned in the Cave of Salamanca (the city where I was born), I could certainly dine exceedingly well at the expense of my heirs ...[197] And I may just make use of it this once, considering the plight I'm in. But I don't know whether these ladies will be as discreet as I have been.

PANCRACIO: You need not concern yourself about them, my friend. Just do as you please and I'll make sure they hold their tongues. I'm very eager to see some of these things you say you've learned in the Cave of Salamanca.

STUDENT: Would you be satisfied if I conjured up two devils for you in human form, carrying a hamper full of good things to eat?

LEONARDA: Devils in my house and in my presence! Sweet Jesus, deliver me from evil!

CRISTINA: This student is Satan himself! Let us pray that some good will come of this ill wind! My heart is all a-flutter.

PANCRACIO: Well, now, if it can be managed without danger and without alarming us, I would very much like to see these devils and their hamper. But I insist, these apparitions must not cause any alarm.

STUDENT: They will appear in the form of the parish sexton and his friend the barber.

CRISTINA: Do you mean Sexton Reponce and Master Roque, the family barber? Poor creatures if they have to be turned into devils! Tell me, friend, will these be baptised devils?

STUDENT: That's something new! Where the devil can you find baptised devils? Or what's the point of baptising devils? All the same, it may be that these devils are baptised, for after all every rule has an exception. Stand aside and I promise that you'll see something truly amazing!

LEONARDA: (aside) Alas, what a calamity! We're quite undone. Our misdoings will be public knowledge. It will be the death of me.

CRISTINA: *(aside)* Courage, madam. Let's put a good face on a bad business.

STUDENT: How now you villains: come forth from the dark.[198]
            Where you are hiding for fear of reproach.
            Come forth and bring with you – do not delay –
            The hamper that's filled with meat and with wine.
            Do not defy me or make me invoke
            Spells, conjurations more harsh and extreme.
            Come forth, I command you. O, why do you stay?
            Heed now my warning, for if you delay
            It will go ill with you. Mark what I say!

Well, now. I know how to deal with these human devils. I must go in alone and cast a spell that's strong enough to bring them out quickly. All the same, with these devils persuasion works better than any spell.

                                            [*Exit the* STUDENT]

PANCRACIO: I wager that if he manages to do as he promises it will be the most extraordinary thing the world has ever seen.

LEONARDA: Of course he'll manage to do it. Why would he disappoint us?

CRISTINA: There's something going on in there. I declare he's bringing them out! Look, there he comes with the devils and that blessed hamper!

        Enter the STUDENT *with the* SEXTON *and the* BARBER.

LEONARDA: Dear Lord! What an amazing resemblance to Sexton Reponce and our good neighbour the barber!

CRISTINA: Take care, madam. You shouldn't take the Lord's name in vain when devils are about.

SEXTON: Say whatever you please. We're like watchdogs who sleep through the storm: nothing alarms us.[199]

LEONARDA: Come over here, I beg you, and let me taste something from that hamper.

STUDENT: I'll be the first to take the risk: I'll make a start on the wine. *(Tastes it)* It's excellent. Is it from Esquivias,[200] my worthy devil from the sacristy?

SEXTON: Indeed it is, I swear by Al . . .

STUDENT: Hold your tongue. Go no further. I'm no friend of devils who swear. Besides, we're not here to commit any mortal sins.[201] We're here to enjoy ourselves and to dine well, with God's blessing.

CRISTINA: Are they going to dine with us?

PANCRACIO: That's right. Devils never eat!

BARBER: Oh, some do and some don't; but we're the eating kind.

CRISTINA: Good sirs, let the poor devils stay since they have brought the dinner. It would hardly be polite to let them starve. After all, they look honest and well behaved.

LEONARDA: They are welcome to stay – if my husband agrees – and as long as they don't frighten us.

PANCRACIO: Let them stay then, for I want to see what I've never seen before.

BARBER: May the good Lord repay you all for your charity!

CRISTINA: What good breeding! What manners! Upon my life, if all devils are like these, from now on they will be my friends!

SEXTON: Then listen all of you and I'll give you true cause to be happy.

> (The SEXTON *plays the guitar and sings, while the*
> BARBER *helps him out with the last line of each*
> *verse.*)[202]

SEXTON: Ignorant people, hear my words.
                 Spoken plainly, freely too.
                 I'll tell you of the virtues hidden
BARBER: In the *Magic Cave of Salamanca*
SEXTON: A famous chronicler set it down
                 On sheets of parchment, old and brown,
                 Cut from the haunch of a frisky mare,
                 Or so they say (be that as it may),
                 This chronicle sings extravagant praise
BARBER: Of the *Magic Cave of Salamanca*.
SEXTON: To study there come rich and poor
                 And those whose wits are failing:
                 They all come out with wiser heads,
                 Replete with useful knowledge;
                 Whilst those who teach there take their seats
                 On benches stained with tarry oil:
                 An arsenal of blackest arts
BARBER: Is the *Magic Cave of Salamanca*.
SEXTON: A never-ending source of wisdom
                 For all who seek. The questing Moor,
                 Even the dullard student finds
                 His head is filled with newfound lore.

	Whoever seeks to study there
	Will nothing lack and nothing rue
BARBER:	In the *Magic Cave of Salamanca*.
SEXTON:	And as for you, our dear Magician,
	In whatever land you call your own,
	You justly merit to be blessed
	With fertile vineyards, red and white.
	If any devil disagrees,
	Then let him first be soundly whipped
	And after never let him enter
BARBER:	*The Magic Cave of Salamanca*.

CRISTINA: Enough of that! Are devils poets too?

BARBER: Yes, and poets are devils.

PANCRACIO: Tell me, sir, since you devils know everything: where did all those scandalous dances come from: the Saraband, the Sambapalo and that newfangled Escarramán?[203]

BARBER: Where? From Hell . . . that's where they come from.

PANCRACIO: That's what I thought.

LEONARDA: I have to admit that I'm quite partial to those wicked dances – except that I don't dare dance them out of concern for my modesty and reputation.

SEXTON: If I were to teach you four new steps a day for a week, you'd be the belle of the ball! I know you are good at it already.

STUDENT: All in good time. Just now dinner is more important.

PANCRACIO: Let us go in. I want to find out whether devils can eat or not, as well as a thousand other things that I've heard about them. I swear to God they shan't leave this house until they have taught me everything there is to be learned in the *Magic Cave of Salamanca*!

THE JEALOUS
OLD MAN

Like *The Magic Cave of Salamanca*, this Interlude is also about deceiving a husband who is old and jealous. Similarly, it draws dramatic and comic tension from the confrontation of two or more groups of characters. As Jean Canavaggio points out, *The Magic Cave* begins with a triangle formed by husband, wife and maid; this gives way to a foursome, comprising the two women and their lovers, abetted by the student, who ultimately manipulates both structures.[204] In *The Jealous Old Man* the structure is simpler: the triangle of husband, wife and cousin (another Cristina) is immediately confronted by the trio of women formed by the wife, her cousin and the bawd, Mistress Ortigosa. The lover who is brought to the house as a result of their scheming remains virtually unseen, except to convince the audience of his actual presence, while the husband thinks that his wife is fooling him.

The plot somewhat resembles that of an Italian *commedia dell'arte* play with the same title (*Il Vecchio Geloso*): the servant, Pedrolino, tricks his master, Pantaleone, by concealing Orazio in a peasant's cottage to which the wife, Isabella, retires to rest after the village festivities. Pantaleone actually connives at his own cuckolding by guarding the door while the lovers are inside.[205]

An even closer parallel exists between this Interlude and Cervantes's Exemplary Novel, *The Jealous Extremaduran*. The plot of the short story, however, is both fuller and more subtle. It also ends tragically on a note of ambiguity, leaving the reader with some sympathy for the husband, who comes to recognise his own responsibility for what has happened. Whereas in an earlier version of the novel Lorenza apparently consents to her seduction, the 1613 text departs radically from this conventional plot line and, instead, maintains her innocence.[206]

The Interlude treats the plot in a cruder, more direct way, without any attempt to suggest ambiguity, or to elicit sympathy for the husband. In keeping with tradition, he is wholly deserving of ridicule. Lorenza is an innocent young wife trapped into marriage with a tiresome, impotent old man; she gladly accepts Mistress Ortigosa's help in fooling her husband, and when she gets her way she shamelessly flaunts her adultery. This is the stuff of traditional comedy, and the audience could be expected to respond accordingly.

It has been suggested that, because of its skeletal treatment of the plot, *The Jealous Old Man* was written after *The Jealous Extremaduran*; even, perhaps, that it was one of the two Interludes hastily composed and added after 1613.[207] On the other hand, the similarity with the plot of the Italian *commedia dell'arte* version and with other Spanish sources suggests an earlier date and lends support to the theory that the novel in its final form is the later, more reflective, elaboration.

CAST

LORENZA
CRISTINA
ORTIGOSA
CAÑIZARES
FRIEND
YOUNG MAN
CONSTABLE
MUSICIANS
DANCER

THE JEALOUS OLD MAN

(El viejo celoso)

Enter LORENZA, *her maid* CRISTINA *and her neighbour*
ORTIGOSA.

LORENZA: It's a miracle, Mistress Ortigosa, that my ball and
chain, the despair and scourge of my life, for once hasn't
turned the key on me. This is the first time since I married
him that I've managed to talk to anyone outside the house.
I'd like to see him dead – along with the wretch who married
me off to him!

ORTIGOSA: Come, Mistress Lorenza, don't complain so. Don't
you know that an old pot may pay for a new one?

LORENZA: They fooled me with that promise and all the other
moonshine too. A curse on his blessed money (I don't mean
to be blasphemous):[208] a pox on his jewels and his fine clothes;
a curse on his gifts and promises of more to come! What use
are they to me if I'm poor in the midst of riches and starve
while others feast?

CRISTINA: That's very true, Aunt. As for me, I'd rather be
dressed in rags and married to a young husband than bur-
dened with that rotten old man you took for a husband.

LORENZA: Did you say that *I* took him, Niece? He was foisted
onto me when I was still a girl and more inclined to obey than
to protest. If I'd had any experience in the matter, I'd have
bitten my tongue off before I said yes – three little letters that
bring a lifetime of misery! But I thought that was the way it
had to be, that there's no preventing the inevitable.

CRISTINA: Jesus! What a disgusting old man! All night long it's
'Bring me the bed pan, empty the bed pan; get up Cristinica
and fetch me hot cloths, my belly's killing me.' Or, 'Where
are my pills? My kidney stone's playing me up.' There are
more salves and potions in his room than you'd find in an
apothecary's shop. As for me, I'm scarcely old enough to dress
myself, yet I have to nurse him. Cluck, cluck, cluck, he coddles

his aches and pains like an old broody hen! I don't know
which makes him more impotent, his hernia or his jealousy!

LORENZA: My niece is quite right.

CRISTINA: I only wish I weren't!

ORTIGOSA: Well, Mistress Lorenza, you just do as I suggest and
you'll see how much better off you'll be! The boy's like a
green sapling; he's willing enough and knows how to hold his
tongue and show his gratitude for favours received. Since the
old man's fits of jealousy and suspicion leave us no room for
manoeuvring, we must proceed with courage and determina-
tion. According to our agreement, madam, I'm to bring the
young gentleman to your bedroom and remove him later –
even if it turns out the old man has more eyes than Argos and
is sharper than a mole underground.[209]

LORENZA: As this is my first time, I'm afraid to risk my good
name for the sake of indulging myself.

CRISTINA: Aunt, that reminds me of that well-known song:

> Mr Gómez Arias,
> Take pity I implore,
> I'm young and sweet and never tried
> To play this game before.[210]

LORENZA: The things you say, Niece! You must be possessed
by an evil spirit!

CRISTINA: I don't know what possesses me – but I do know
that I'd go along with everything Mistress Ortigosa has
suggested, without skipping a single detail.

LORENZA: What about my honour, Niece?

CRISTINA: What about our fun, Aunt?

LORENZA: What if we're found out?

CRISTINA: What if we're not?

LORENZA: How can I be sure that we won't be?

ORTIGOSA: How you can be sure? Why, as long as you're
quick, clever and careful ... above all, be of good courage
and trust me.

CRISTINA: See here, Mistress Ortigosa, go fetch the gentleman
and let him be perfect, cheerful, a touch bold and, above all,
young!

ORTIGOSA: He has all those qualities, plus two more: he's
wealthy and generous too!

LORENZA: I don't need his wealth, Mistress Ortigosa: I'm
loaded with jewels and quite overcome by all the colours of

my extensive wardrobe. Cañizares can take credit for that – he keeps me dressed to the nines, with more jewels than you'd see in a silversmith's shop. It's not just my virtue he's guarding when he seals the doors and windows, patrols the house at all hours, and chases away all the male cats and dogs. I'd gladly forego his gifts and favours to be done with all that and his other unheard-of precautions as well.

ORTIGOSA: He's as jealous as that?

LORENZA: I should say so! Why the other day he was offered a piece of tapestry at a bargain price, but he turned it down because it was decorated with human figures; instead, he paid extra for one with a floral design, even though it was of poorer quality. You have to go through seven doors before you get to my room (and that's not counting the street door): every one is locked and I can't find out where he keeps the keys at night.

CRISTINA: Aunt, I think he keeps the master key under his nightshirt.

LORENZA: Don't you believe it, Niece. I sleep with him and there's never a sign of anything under there!

CRISTINA: What's more, all night long he wanders through the house like a ghost. If he hears anyone playing music in the street he'll throw stones until they go away. He's wicked, he's an ogre, he's an old man – need I say more?

LORENZA: You'd better leave now, Mistress Ortigosa, for if the old fusspot comes and finds you here we're done for. Let's do what we agreed without further delay, for I'm so desperate I'm ready to put a rope around my neck and end this terrible life I'm leading.

ORTIGOSA: Perhaps what's about to happen will banish that black thought and you'll lead a healthier, happier life.

CRISTINA: I'd give my right hand if that would help. I dearly love my aunt and it pains me to see her so downcast and miserable in the clutches of that old, old, that older than old man – I can't stop calling him 'old'!

LORENZA: But Cristina, he's really very fond of you.

CRISTINA: Does that make him any less old? Besides, I've heard that old men are always fond of young girls.

ORTIGOSA: That's true, Cristina. And now goodbye. I'll be back after dinner. Madam, have faith in our plan and you'll see how well it'll turn out.

CRISTINA: Mistress Ortigosa, please do me a favour and bring me a little friar for me to play with.

ORTIGOSA: The young lady shall have one as pretty as a picture.

CRISTINA: I don't want a picture. I want a real live one, a nice juicy little fellow.

LORENZA: What if your uncle should see him?

CRISTINA: I'll tell him it's a ghost, that way he'll be scared and I'll have my fun.

ORTIGOSA: I'll bring him to you. I must leave you for a while.

[ORTIGOSA *exits*]

CRISTINA: Listen, Aunt: if Ortigosa brings your young man and my little friar and the master sees them, all we have to do is jump on him together and strangle him; then we'll throw him in the well or bury him in the stable.

LORENZA: If I know you, you'll be as good as your word.

CRISTINA: Well, the old man shouldn't be jealous. Why can't he leave us in peace? We do him no harm and we live like saints.

[*They exit.*]

Enter the old man, CAÑIZARES, *and his* FRIEND.

CAÑIZARES: See here my good friend, when a man in his seventies marries a girl of fifteen, either he's out of his mind or he's in a hurry to move on to the next world. I'd scarcely wed little Mistress Lorenza, expecting to find in her my joy and companion – someone to be at my bedside to close my eyes when I die – when I was beset by a whole host of trials and vexations.

I surrendered my house when I took me a spouse,
Gave up the quiet life when I found me a wife.

FRIEND: It was indeed a mistake, my friend, but not a serious one, for as the Bible says, 'It's better to marry than to burn.'[211]

CAÑIZARES: Why, there was so little left in me to burn that the smallest flame would have reduced me to ashes! A mate is what I wanted, a mate is what I looked for, and a mate is what I found. Now it's in God's hands . . .

FRIEND: Are you jealous, my friend?

CAÑIZARES: Of the sun that shines on my little Lorenza, of the air she breathes, even of her skirts when they brush against her legs.

FRIEND: Does she give you cause to be jealous?

CAÑIZARES: Not in the least, and I don't give her any opportunity to do so. The windows are locked, shuttered and barred; the doors are never opened; as long as I live, not even a female neighbour shall cross the threshold. Mark you, women don't get the wrong ideas from going out on high days and feast days and to other public celebrations. No, where they come to grief and fall from grace is in the house next door, with other women friends. A false friend keeps more things hidden than a dark night. More plots are conceived and delivered in that friend's house than in any public place.

FRIEND: I'm of the same opinion. All the same, if Mistress Lorenza never leaves the house and no one enters it either, how is it you are still not satisfied, my friend?

CAÑIZARES: I'm afraid that Lorenza may soon find out what she's missing. That would be terrible – so terrible that I'm frightened just to think about it. My fear drives me to desperation and so my life is miserable.

FRIEND: You're right to be afraid: wives like to enjoy the full fruits of marriage.

CAÑIZARES: My wife enjoys them with diminishing returns.

FRIEND: Ah, there's the rub, my friend.

CAÑIZARES: No, no, that's unthinkable. Lorenza is as innocent as a dove, and so far she understands nothing of such goings-on. Now farewell, my friend, I must go in.

FRIEND: I should like to go in with you and see Mistress Lorenza.

CAÑIZARES: I'll have you know, sir, there's an old Latin saying, 'Amicus usque ad aras', which means 'Friendship as far as the altar': in other words, a man must do everything for his friend except what offends God. So I say 'usque ad portam', 'Friendship as far as the door'. No one crosses my threshold. Farewell my friend, and forgive me.

CAÑIZARES *goes into the house.*

FRIEND: Never in my life have I seen a man who was so cautious, so jealous or so unreasonable! He'll be hoist with his own petard and die of the very sickness he dreads so much.

[CAÑIZARES *exits.*]

Enter LORENZA *and* CRISTINA.

CRISTINA: Aunt, Uncle's late and Ortigosa's even later.

LORENZA: I wish neither of them would come, for he makes me angry and she has me all confused.

CRISTINA: Aunt, the proof of the pudding is in the eating. If it doesn't turn out right, throw it out.

LORENZA: Just a moment, Niece! If I know anything about these matters, the eating is the dangerous part.

CRISTINA: Good grief, Aunt, you're not very brave. If I were your age, even armed men wouldn't scare me!

LORENZA: If I've said it once, I'll say it a hundred times, you have the devil in your tongue! Oh Lord, how did the master get in?

CRISTINA: He must have used the master key.

LORENZA: The devil take this master, with his tricks and his keys!

Enter CAÑIZARES.

CAÑIZARES: Who were you talking to, Mistress Lorenza?

LORENZA: I was talking to Cristinica.

CAÑIZARES: Take care, Mistress Lorenza.

LORENZA: I said I was talking to Cristinica. Who else would I be talking to? Do I have any choice?

CAÑIZARES: I wouldn't want you to be saying something unpleasant about me, even to yourself.

LORENZA: I can't make out your riddles, nor do I want to. That's enough of that!

CAÑIZARES: More than enough! I don't want to quarrel with you. Who's that knocking so loudly at the door? Go and see, Cristinica. If it's a beggar, give him some money and send him on his way.

CRISTINA: Who's there?

ORTIGOSA: Cristina, it's Mistress Ortigosa.

CAÑIZARES: Mistress Ortigosa, our neighbour? Lord love us! Ask her what she wants, Cristina, and give it to her – but make sure she doesn't come into the house.

CRISTINA: What do you want, good neighbour?

CAÑIZARES: The word neighbour disturbs me. Call her by her name, Cristina.

CRISTINA: Answer me, Mistress Ortigosa. What do you want?

ORTIGOSA: I have a request to make of Master Cañizares. It's a matter of life and death, not to mention honour.

CAÑIZARES: Niece, tell the lady that keeping her out of this house is also a matter of life and death, not to mention honour.

LORENZA: Lord, how you do carry on! Aren't I standing beside you? Can she devour me with her eyes, or whisk me off on a broomstick?

CAÑIZARES: By all the devils, let her come in, since you insist!

CRISTINA: Come in, neighbour.

CAÑIZARES: That word neighbour is a bad omen.

ORTIGOSA *enters carrying a roll of leather embossed at the four corners with the figures of Mandricardo, Rugero, Gradosa, Rodamonte – Rodamonte depicted in his cloak.*[212]

ORTIGOSA: Most revered sir, prompted by your honour's good reputation, your charity and your generous almsgiving, I make so bold as to implore of you a particularly charitable and generous favour: please buy this tapestry. You see, my son's in prison for wounding a tanner. The court has ordered the surgeon to make a sworn statement, but I have no money to buy him off – and there's a risk they'll make him pay further costs – substantial ones – because he's a naughty boy, my son. So I'd like to get him out of prison today or tomorrow, if that's possible. This is a fine piece of work and quite new; even so, I'll sell it for whatever your honour cares to give me, for its value is incalculable, like all the things I've lost in this life. Take hold of this corner, madam, and let's unfold it, so that Master Cañizares can see that I'm not deceiving him. Lift it up, madam – see what a fine piece it is when I stretch it out. How lifelike the pictures are!

As they lift the piece of tapestry and display it, a YOUNG MAN *slips in behind it.* CAÑIZARES *looks at the picture.*

CAÑIZARES: Ah, the charming Rodamonte! What's that little fellow in a cloak doing in my house? If he knew how little I care for disguises and that kind of thing, he'd make himself scarce.

CRISTINA: Dear Uncle, I know nothing about anyone in a cloak. If someone has entered the house, then Mistress Ortigosa is to blame. As for me, may the devil carry me off if I've had anything to do with it. No, by my conscience: it would be the devil's business if my dear uncle thought I was guilty!

CAÑIZARES: Indeed, Niece, I can see that Mistress Ortigosa is to blame; but I shouldn't be surprised, for she doesn't know my nature, nor what an enemy I am of those pictures.

LORENZA: He means the pictures, Cristinica, nothing else.

CRISTINA: Of course, that's what I mean, too. (*aside to* LORENZA) Ooh! God's love! I was quite out of my wits, but I'm recovering now!

LORENZA: Keep your big mouth shut! I should have known better than to trust a novice.

CRISTINA: Unhappy me. I nearly upset the apple cart!

CAÑIZARES: Mistress Ortigosa, I'm not interested in figures, cloaked or otherwise. Take this coin, it will take care of your needs. Now, leave my house as fast as you can. The sooner the better, and take your tapestry with you.

ORTIGOSA: God grant you live longer, sir, than old Methal-in-the-Cellar,[213] and madam too – I don't know her name. Please tell her that I'm at her command, ready to serve her day and night, with body and soul. Why, her soul must be as pure as a turtledove's.

CAÑIZARES: Mistress Ortigosa, be brief and be gone. Don't be so quick to judge the souls of others.

ORTIGOSA: If my lady has need of any poultices for the mothering complaint, I have some miraculous ones; or if she suffers from toothache, I know a charm that will make the pain vanish very handily.[214]

CAÑIZARES: That will do, Mistress Ortigosa, Madam Lorenza has neither mother or toothache. Her teeth are all healthy and sound – perfectly intact.

ORTIGOSA: She'll lose everything in good time if she lives long enough. After all, old age is very hard on the teeth.

CAÑIZARES: May the Lord deliver us! Is there no way to get rid of this neighbour? Ortigosa, neighbour, or devil, or whatever you are, go with God's blessing and leave me here in peace.

ORTIGOSA: That's a reasonable request. Don't worry, sir, I'm off.

[*She exits*]

CAÑIZARES: Neighbours, neighbours! I'm still suspicious of that woman's kind words. Once burned, twice shy.

LORENZA: I think you're a brute and a savage. What has our neighbour said that you treat her so unkindly? Even when you do something generous you commit a mortal sin. With

one hand you shower her with coins, while you heap curses
on her with the other! You have the tongue of a cat or a
scorpion! You're a cesspool of spite and malice!

CAÑIZARES: No, no, that's not so, I just don't like the way the
wind is blowing – you're too quick to defend your neighbour.

CRISTINA: Aunt, come inside and calm yourself. Leave Uncle
alone, he seems to be in a bad mood.

LORENZA: That I will, Niece, and he shan't see my face for the
next two hours. Indeed, I'll make him swallow his words,
whether or not he likes it.

[LORENZA *exits*]

CRISTINA: There, Uncle, you see how she slammed the door? I
think she's gone to find a bar to make it fast.

LORENZA, *in the next room.*

LORENZA: Are you there, Cristinica?

CRISTINA: What's the matter, Aunt?

LORENZA: You should see the gentleman my good fortune has
brought me! He's young and good-looking, with black hair.
His breath smells like orange blossom.

CRISTINA: Dear Lord, what madness and folly! Aunt, are you
out of your mind?

LORENZA: No, I'm perfectly sane. Truly, if you could see him,
you'd jump for joy.

CRISTINA: Dear Lord, what madness and folly! Tell her off,
Uncle, she ought not to say such naughty things, even in fun.

CAÑIZARES: What nonsense are you babbling, Lorenza? I'll
have you know I'm not in the mood for jokes.

LORENZA: This is far from being a joke. So far, in fact, that it
couldn't go any further!

CRISTINA: Dear Lord, what madness and folly! Tell me, Aunt,
is my little friar there too?

LORENZA: No, Niece, he isn't. But he'll come next time, if
neighbour Ortigosa is willing.

CAÑIZARES: Lorenza, say what you will, but stop using that
word neighbour. Just to hear it I'm all of a tremble.

LORENZA: Thanks to the neighbour, I'm all of a tremble too.

CRISTINA: Dear Lord, what madness and folly!

LORENZA: Now I see you for what you are, wretched old man.
Until now the life I've lived with you has been a sham!

CRISTINA: Scold her, Uncle, scold her, do. She's quite
shameless!

LORENZA: I want a bowl of angelica water to wash a young gentleman's beard ... such as it is. He has the face of an angel in a painting.

CRISTINA: Dear Lord ... you should tear her to pieces, Uncle.

CAÑIZARES: I shan't tear her to pieces – just the door that keeps her from me.

LORENZA: There's no need. See, it's open. Come in and you'll see that everything I've said is true.

CAÑIZARES: I'll come in to please you, although I know it's just a joke.

> As CAÑIZARES *enters, they throw a bowl of water in his face. He stops to dry his eyes and* CRISTINA *and* LORENZA *crowd round him. At that moment, the* YOUNG MAN *slips out.*

CAÑIZARES: For God's sake, you almost blinded me, Lorenza. Tricks played on the eyes are the devil's work.

LORENZA: It's just my luck to be married to the most suspicious man in the world! See how his wretched jealousy made him believe my lies. I'm the one who's wretched and out of luck! I'll pay for what this old man has done with the hairs of my head; my eyes will weep for the faults he has committed! Look what's become of my honour and my credit. After all, suspicions lead to certainties, and lies to truths; jokes become realities and pleasures turn to curses. Ah, I'm torn asunder.

CRISTINA: Aunt, don't make such a noise, you'll bring the whole neighbourhood.

CONSTABLE: (*off stage*) Open up these doors. Open them at once or I'll break them down.

LORENZA: Open them wide, Cristinica! Let everyone hear of my innocence and this old man's wickedness!

CAÑIZARES: God forgive me, Lorenza, I thought you were joking. Do be quiet!

> *Enter the* CONSTABLE *with the* MUSICIANS, *a* DANCER *and* ORTIGOSA.

CONSTABLE: What's this? What are you quarrelling about? Who was shouting here?

CAÑIZARES: It's nothing, sir. A quarrel between husband and wife – it's soon over.

MUSICIANS: God's life, my fellow musicians and I were at a wedding close by. We came when we heard the shouts; all alarmed we were, thinking it was something serious.

ORTIGOSA: Me too, sinful soul that I am.

CAÑIZARESA: Well, Mistress Ortigosa, if it hadn't been for you, none of this would have happened.

ORTIGOSA: My sins are to blame. It's my misfortune that, without knowing the whys and wherefores, I'm blamed for the faults of others.

CAÑIZARES: I'd be obliged, sirs, if you'd leave us now. I thank you for your good offices; my wife and I have made peace with each other.

LORENZA: I'll keep the peace on condition you ask the neighbour to forgive you for harbouring any unkind thoughts against her.

CAÑIZARES: If I had to ask forgiveness of all the neighbours I've thought about unkindly, there'd be no end to it. All the same, I do ask Mistress Ortigosa to forgive me.

ORTIGOSA: I forgive you here and now. Let's say no more about it.

MUSICIANS: Well, we can't say we came here for nothing, so my friends will play a tune, the dancer will perform and we'll celebrate your peacemaking with this song.

CAÑIZARES: Gentlemen, I don't want any music. I shall consider your duties already discharged.

MUSICIANS: Well, even though you don't want it . . .

They sing.

The rain that falls on Midsummer's Day
Weakens the wine and spoils the hay.
    Quarrels in June at the Feast of St John
    The rest of the year are forgotten and gone.[215]
When wheat is golden, full and fine,
The grapes are scanty on the vine,
The farmer's barns may overflow
While yet his casks in wine are low.
A quarrel that seems bound to grow,
    If it falls in June at the Feast of St John
    The rest of the year is forgotten and gone.

The summer sun is hot and bright
And men are quick to pick a fight,
But later when the trees are bare
The tempers cool and scarcely flare,

So listen now and have a care:
> Quarrels in June at the Feast of St John
> The rest of the year are forgotten and gone.

When married couples shout and spat,
Then let it be no worse than that,
So when their anger's safely spent,
Without a grudge they'll live content.
The sun returning after rain
Brings greater comfort after pain.
> Quarrels in June at the Feast of St John
> The rest of the year are forgotten and gone.

CAÑIZARES: So you see, good sirs, what confusion and turmoil this neighbour has caused me and how right I am to be wary of my neighbours.

LORENZA: Although my husband mistrusts you, dear neighbours, I embrace you, one and all.

CRISTINA: And so do I. Still, I would have thought better of my neighbour if she'd brought me my little friar. Farewell, dear neighbours.

NOTES

In compiling these Notes I am indebted to the following editions of Cervantes's *Entremeses* in Spanish:

Eugenio Asensio: *Cervantes: Entremeses* (Madrid: Castalia, 1970).

J. B. Avalle-Arce: *Ocho entremeses* (Englewood Cliffs, New Jersey: Prentice-Hall, 1970).

Adolfo Bonilla y San Martín: *Entremeses* . . . (Madrid: Asociación de la librería de España, 1916).

Jean Canavaggio: *Entremeses* (Madrid: Taurus, 1982).

Miguel de Cervantes: *Ocho comedias, y ocho entremeses nuevos, nunca representados: facsímil de la primera edición* (Madrid: Real Academia Española, 1984).

Miguel Herrero García. *Entremeses* . . . (Madrid: Espasa-Calpe, 1945).

Rodolfo Schevill and Adolfo Bonilla: *Entremeses* in *Obras completas de Miguel de Cervantes Saavedra*, vol. IV (Madrid: 1915–22).

Florencio Sevilla Arroyo and Antonio Rey Hazas: In *Teatro completo* (Barcelona: Planeta, 1987).

Nicholas Spadaccini: *Entremeses* (Madrid: Cátedra, 1982).

I am also indebted to the following:

Eugenio Asensio: *Itinerario del entremés: desde Lope de Rueda a Quiñones de Benavente* (Madrid: Gredos, 1965).

Autoridades: Diccionario de la lengua castellana . . . *compuesto por la Real Academia Española*, (1726–39) 6 vols. (Madrid: Gredos, 1964).

Covarrubias: Sebastián de Covarrubias: *Tesoro de la lengua castellana o española* (Madrid, 1611), ed. Martín de Riquer (Barcelona: S. A. Horta, 1943).

Miguel Herrero García: *Ideas de los españoles del siglo XVII* (Madrid: Gredos, 1966).

Maurice Molho: *Cervantes: raíces folklóricas* (Madrid: Gredos, 1976).

Other references are listed under 'Suggestions for Further Reading'.

1 The Prologue appears at the beginning of the 1615 edition, together with other preliminaries and a dedication addressed to the Conde de Lemos. The Interludes are preceded by Eight Plays: *El gallardo español* (*The Gallant Spaniard*); *La casa de los celos* (*The House of Jealousy*); *Los baños de Argel* (*The Bagnios of Algiers*); *El rufián dichoso* (*The Fortunate Scoundrel*); *La gran sultana* (*The Grand Sultana*); *El laberinto de amor* (*The Labyrinth of Love*); *La entretenida* (*The Comedy of Entertainment*); and *Pedro de Urdemalas*.

2 Lope de Rueda died in 1565. He followed the example of Italian acting companies (whose performances he probably saw in the 1530s) by forming his own company and performing secular and religious plays throughout Spain. In 1552 he was engaged by the city council of Valladolid to write and perform plays during Corpus Christi festivities; this was almost certainly the first permanent theatrical appointment of its kind in Spain and anticipated the later establishment of commercial playhouses.

3 In 1603 Agustín de Rojas published a vivid description of the lives of such strolling players in *El viaje entretenido* (*The Entertaining Journey*), translated in A. M. Nagler, *A Source Book in Theatrical History* (New York: Dover Books, 1959), pp. 57–60.

4 Agustín de Rojas also refers to a man called Navarro, 'a native of Toledo – who was the first to invent theatrical effects ("teatros")'. Nothing else is known of this man.

5 *Life in Algiers* (*El trato de Argel*) and *The Siege of Numantia* (*La destrucción de Numancia*) were written during the 1580s, before Lope de Vega established the new fashion in theatrical taste. *The Naval Battle* (*La batalla naval*) has disappeared without trace.

6 The claim of being the first to write plays in three acts instead of four is dubious, and disputed by other playwrights such as Cristóbal de Virués. Cervantes's claim to be the first to show allegorical characters ('figurs morales') on stage is also questionable unless this is taken to mean that he was the first to use them to express inner thoughts and feelings (Canavaggio, *Cervantes*, p.120). Cervantes's boast that he wrote 'some twenty or thirty plays' during the 1580s is also thought to be exaggerated. Today, only ten full-length plays are known to be his.

7 While Lope himself claimed he had written fifteen hundred plays, his friend Juan Pérez de Montalbán put the figure at eighteen hundred. The

actual number was probably somewhere between seven and eight hundred.

8 The playwrights named here were all contemporaries of Cervantes and most probably known to him personally.

9 The number of acting companies licensed by royal decree to perform plays in public was strictly limited. In 1615 there were twelve such companies, and before that only eight.

10 The bookseller was Juan de Villarroel.

11 *Deceptive Appearances* (*El engaño a los ojos*) is another of Cervantes's plays of which nothing is now known; it is likely that he never managed to complete it.

12 Spadaccini/Talens, *Through the Shattering Glass*, pp. 33–4.

13 Asensio, *Entremeses*, p. 40. On the other hand, Mary Gaylord Randel makes a convincing case for finding an implicit logic and purpose in this apparent disorder.

14 *El teatro de Cervantes*, p. 307.

15 For a discussion of this pessimistic view of life, see J. A. Maravall, *Culture of the Baroque*, pp. 194–204.

16 The Spanish word 'vejete' indicates that this old man is meant to be a figure of fun. *Autoridades* specifically defines it as meaning 'a ridiculous old man, like those found in Interludes or satirical one-act plays'.

17 A reference to an exemption from taxes applied to certain hunting birds.

18 It was the custom to enter into contracts for a period of three years.

19 This is probably a dig at those economic advisers (known as 'arbitristas') whose warnings of impending disaster were frequently ridiculed.

20 The old man says that he has never *confessed* anything – a word often used in picaresque jargon to mean that he never 'squealed' to the authorities (i.e. he never denounced his wife despite the torture of their marriage).

21 According to civil law in seventeenth-century Spain, all property

acquired by a couple during their marriage was regarded as jointly owned.

22 An allusion to Cervantes's captivity in North Africa. It was not unusual to find Calabrians serving in the Turkish galleys (see *Don Quixote* I, 39).

23 Women in convents were protected from the outside world by grilles and turnstiles. All visits were supervised and the conversation reported to the Prioress.

24 A reference to the words of Pontius Pilate when he refused to condemn Jesus: 'Quia nullam invenio causam' (John 18, 38). The English translation is from the King James version.

25 A well-groomed soldier did not fit popular expectation. The shabby suitor in *Sir Vigilant* was much closer to the comic stereotype.

26 In Cervantes's time the Guadalajara Gate was the main entrance to Madrid. The streets surrounding it were filled with shops selling quality goods: silk and brocade, precious stones and jewellery, silver and gold. It was also a popular meeting place.

27 *Autoridades* notes that among those who frequented the gaming houses 'some went to play cards, others to amuse themselves and the rest to earn a quick tip – these were called onlookers ("mirones")'. They earned their money by assisting the players in various ways, presumably mostly fraudulent, since Guiomar claims that they were unpopular with the owners of the gaming houses. (See *Don Quixote* II, 49.)

28 These men could afford only one suit, of the kind worn in the streets of the city. According to Avalle-Arce, this suit was black, whereas it was customary to change into more colourful clothes for travelling, or for wear in the country. How comic, then, is the description of these petty officials riding on mules in their city clothes, wearing cloth leggings instead of riding boots, and with only one spur (which undoubtedly would have made the mule go round in circles)!

29 This bridge crosses the Manzanares River on the southern side of Madrid, on the road to Toledo.

30 In seventeenth-century Europe a barber was also called upon to perform routine medical tasks. Since the stage directions specifically indicate that the barber-surgeon enters 'dressed as a doctor', no doubt the audience would have laughed at his pretentiousness. Cervantes's own father was also a barber-surgeon (see Introduction).

31 The hood consisted of four pieces of cloth sewn together to form a point at the back of the head.

32 Bonilla claims that many who worked as porters were of Morisco or Jewish descent, hence the insistence by this character that he is a true Christian. The reference in the next sentence to the brotherhood of labourers makes fun of the fact that porters ('ganapanes') were often called 'working brothers' ('hermanos del trabajo') (*Covarrubias* s.v. 'Ganapán').

33 Sancho observes in a letter to Don Quixote that 'it is a common opinion in this town ... that there is not a worse sort of people than your market-women. For they are a shameless, godless, brazen lot, as I can well believe from my experience of other places' (*Don Quixote* II, 51).

34 The porter compares the swift action of his sword to a 'sackbut' ('sacabuche'), a kind of bass trombone with a metal slide. According to Covarrubias, anyone not aware of how this instrument functioned might think it was issuing from the player's stomach!

35 The heavy demand for wood as a source of fuel meant that it was in short supply in Europe in the sixteenth and seventeenth centuries (Fernand Braudel, *The Structures of Everyday Life* I, tr. Sian Reynolds, [New York: Harper and Row, 1981], p. 366). The porter's offer therefore represents a substantial bribe.

36 A quotation from a well-known Spanish proverb: 'las riñas de por San Juan son paz para todo el año' ('squabble at the time of the Feast of St John and you'll live in peace the rest of the year'). It refers to the custom of renting houses and hiring new servants in June (the Feast of St John is celebrated on 24 June) and implies that once the haggling and signing of the contract are over, no one needs to worry about it for another year. A reference to this proverb also appears in the refrain of the song that closes *The Jealous Old Man*.

37 After 1600 there was a preference for writing Interludes in verse, probably in imitation of the *Comedia*.

38 Luis Vélez de Guevara, in his allegorical novel *El diablo cojuelo* (*The Lame Devil*).

39 See Zimic, *El teatro de Cervantes*, pp. 309–324. The text of Garcilaso's *Eglogas* can be found, with prose translations, in *Renaissance and Baroque Poetry of Spain*, ed. Elias L. Rivers (Prospect Heights: Waveland Press, 1988).

40 According to Asensio, 1612 was a year in which the vogue for Escarramán reached a peak (provoking both fervent support and equally strong condemnation). He argues that this is further evidence for dating the Interlude (*Itinerario*, p. 103).

41 As noted by Nicholas Spadaccini, *Entremeses* (1982), p. 69.

42 The title of Bachelor ('bachiller') indicates that the character in question has graduated from a university. According to *Autoridades*, however, the title was also mockingly bestowed on someone given to irrelevant and empty talk.

43 The concern with racial purity ('Limpieza de sangre') began as a rallying call for the Reconquest of the Peninsula from Arab domination. It became a symbol of Christian superiority over the races with whom Spanish Christians had previously coexisted for remarkably long periods.

44 See Henry Kamen, *Inquisition and Society in Spain in the Sixteenth and Seventeenth Centuries*.

45 For example, the Spanish scholar Francisco Ynduráin believes that Cervantes may have intended it as a prescription for an ideal relationship between Church and State. (See the Prologue to his edition of the *Entremeses* [Madrid, 1962].)

46 It was customary for a widower to wear a long dark cloak, closely fastened down the front.

47 A Latin phrase meaning 'Come with me.' It was also the name given to the pouch in which a student carried his books and, by extension, denoted the student himself.

48 Trampagos calls them 'the dark ones' ('las morenas'). This refers to fencing foils, which were blunt, by contrast with 'las espadas blancas', which had sharp blades and were used for a more deadly purpose.

49 In Cervantes's time a mattress was usually laid on supporting benches; Trampagos later reminds Vademecum to fetch the bench.

50 A reference to a gypsy belief that life could be prolonged by

catching the last breath of a dying person and keeping it in one's stomach.

51 Trampagos refers to the immoral earnings that Pericona paid him while under his protection. In return, a pimp was often called upon to defend the prostitute and to suffer imprisonment and whipping at the hands of the law.

52 During Lent it was customary to direct special sermons to prostitutes, urging them to change their way of life. The French traveller, Antoine de Brunel, noted: 'There is one day devoted to exhorting them to repent. This is on Good Friday when they are taken by several constables to the church of the Recogidas ... there they are placed beneath the preacher's pulpit and he proceeds to do his best to move their hearts; but he rarely succeeds' (*Voyage de l'Espagne curieux, historique et politique. Fait en l'année 1655*).

53 A reference to the stomach. Hypochondria was a fashionable complaint in the seventeenth century.

54 Sweating was part of the treatment prescribed for syphilis. Cf. the opening paragraph of Cervantes's *The Deceitful Marriage* (the Exemplary Tale which serves as introduction to the longer story called *The Dogs' Colloquy*).

55 The royal palace, south of Madrid, famous for its formal gardens in the French and Dutch style. It was especially noted for its fountains and artificial lakes.

56 Vademecum actually refers to these 'ladies' as 'moscovitas' – a play on the word 'moscas' ('flies'), but the pun is lost in translation. The nonsensical names of the prostitutes roughly translate as Repolished, Chuck-Chuckle and Stray.

57 The town of Potosí, in Bolivia, was famous for its silver mines. The next line evokes the image of ivy clinging to a wall.

58 Well known in seventeenth-century Madrid as a place where women gathered to wash laundry in the Manzanares River. It was also the site of a popular tavern.

59 Although these lines are given to Juan in all the editions I have consulted, including the Facsimile of the first edition, it is more logical to give them to Chiquiznaque, otherwise Repulida's ensuing comment is puzzling.

60 Repulida calls Chiquiznaque 'Zonzorino Catón', which is a humorous reference to Cato, the Censor, a Roman author known for his moralising.

61 The allusion here is to a contemporary trick in the form of a box which, when opened, released a metal spring that resembled a snake. Repulida means that Pizpita is as harmless as the toy snake.

62 Pizpita calls her 'Doña Mari-Bobales' and 'monda-níspolas'. The first name includes the word 'boba' – 'idiot'; the second refers to the superfluous act of peeling a plum ('níspola' is the fruit of the medlar tree).

63 Pimps were forbidden by law from carrying on their business; the penalty for breaking the law was deportation.

64 It was the custom to mark slaves by branding the letter 'S' on their faces.

65 The prostitution business was organised according to a strict hierarchy (see Cervantes's account in *Rinconete and Cortadillo*).

66 Barbers were often musicians as well (see also the end of *Sir Vigilant*).

67 A burlesque reference to an ancient marriage custom of somewhat scatalogical nature (Spadaccini, *Entremeses*, p. 132).

68 A fictitious character associated with Spanish picaresque life and made famous by Francisco de Quevedo (1580–1645). A notoriously immoral dance was named after him (see *The Magic Cave of Salamanca*).

69 This account is yet another echo of Cervantes's personal experience at the hands of the Barbary pirates who captured him. It was the custom to place two oarsmen in the stern of the galley to set the pace for the rest of the crew.

70 A monastery in an ancient town in what is now the Province of Logroño.

71 The actual reference is to a well-known ballad attributed to Lope de Vega which begins 'Saddle up the roan pony that belongs to the mayor of Los Vélez' (Spadaccini, *Entremeses*, p. 136).

72 Mostrenca alludes both to applause and to whip lashes (both are meanings of the word 'palmeo').

73 Cervantes evokes two meanings of the verb 'sonar': to be famous and to blow one's nose, with various attendant images.

74 According to legend, the shepherd Erostratos set fire to the temple of Diana in Ephesus (one of the seven wonders of the world) so as to leave an enduring memory of himself.

75 When an extra turn of speed was required from the oarsmen in the galleys, the order given was 'fuera ropa' (literally 'off with your clothes').

76 Coscolina was another prostitute in Quevedo's poems about Escarramán.

77 The dances named in this passage were all considered more or less scandalous in Cervantes's day. (See also *The Magic Cave of Salamanca*.)

78 A knight at the court of the Emperor Charlemagne, Roland's heroic exploits are celebrated in the medieval epic known as *The Song of Roland*.

79 Daganzo is a town near Cervantes's birthplace, Alcalá de Henares. In the seventeenth century it came under the jurisdiction of Toledo.

80 Literally, 'Let us return to the matter.'

81 According to the laws of the ancient kingdom of Toledo, the election of magistrates had to be approved by the feudal landowner.

82 Stringbean actually suggests that the candidates are worthy to govern in Romanillos, a small town in the province of Guadalajara. The absurd linking of two places ridicules Crusty's exaggerated claims.

83 In Spanish the pun depends on the words 'sorbe' ('sip' or 'suck'), and 'orbe' ('orb', 'sphere').

84 Sancho Panza tells an almost identical story in *Don Quixote* II, 13.

85 The wine from Esquivias (a small town near Madrid, in the province of Toledo) was renowned for its excellent quality. It was the town where Cervantes's wife Catalina was born and continued to live during the first twenty years of her marriage, during her husband's long and frequent absences.

86 A reference to some verses about a dog that persisted in barking at Jews.

87 In Spanish the comic play on words involves Crusty's failure to

distinguish between the term 'proto-médicos' (i.e. doctors who acted as examiners for medical students) and 'potra', meaning a hernia.

88 This was a safe way of carrying documents on one's person in the seventeenth century (see *Sir Vigilant*).

89 Puff's outburst reflects the widespread belief in seventeenth-century Spain that educated people were Jewish converts and therefore suspect.

90 The three other prayers were the Ave Maria, the Credo and the Salve Regina. Puff's anxiety to prove that he is a true Christian reflects the contemporary concern with purity of blood (see Introduction).

91 It is clear from Stringbean's previous comment that Knuckleknees is adept with the slingshot! The Spanish text makes the comparison with Catullus, who was a poet rather than a soldier. Like Puff's earlier reference to a Roman senator, the allusion is plainly absurd.

92 Along with doctors or tailors, lawyers were often the object of ridicule in seventeenth-century Spain. Lycurgus was a famous Greek law-giver. In the Spanish text Clod offers to wipe himself with Bártulo – a celebrated legal authority in fourteenth-century Italy.

93 This reference to the famous Roman orator Cato is of the same order as the other comic allusions to Rome and Romans which occur throughout the play.

94 Stringbean insinuates that the notary is a Jewish convert by using the term 'Escriba' (someone who interprets Jewish law). The notary retaliates by calling Stringbean a pharisee, an equally pejorative epithet.

95 The Bachelor means that he has been appointed to organise the local festivities for the feast of Corpus Christi, which falls in late May or early June.

96 Samson was, of course, famous for his strength, and Solomon for his wisdom. By inverting these legendary attributes, the musicians are making fun of the councillors and their absurd examination of the foolish peasant candidates.

97 In the original text Puff confuses the words 'raros' ('rare' or 'unusual') and 'ralos' ('few', 'scanty').

98 Cervantes is quoting a verse from a well-known song that gave its name to a dance called 'el polvillo'. This dance was one of many that were condemned by moral and religious authorities as scandalous and immoral.

99 See *Sir Vigilant*.

100 Crusty quotes a phrase which originally appeared in the chivalresque novel *Amadís de Gaula (Amadis of Gaul)* as a term of challenge. 'Agora lo veredes, dijo Agrajes' later became a familiar cliché in comic literature.

101 See *Sir Vigilant*.

102 It is interesting to compare this scene with *Don Quixote* I, 17, in which Sancho Panza is tossed in a blanket for refusing to pay at the inn. I am grateful to Professor Don Beecher for drawing my attention to the Towneley *Second Shepherd's Pageant*, in which a sheep stealer is punished by a similar tossing.

103 J. P. Wickersham Crawford notes that Cervantes probably borrowed the idea from Juan Timoneda's *Comedia de Amphitrión* (published in 1559). In the Interlude the courtly *questione d'amore* is transposed into the comic key. (See *Spanish Drama Before Lope de Vega*, Philadelphia: University of Pennsylvania Press, 1967, pp. 122–4.) Other critics see a parallel with an Italian farcical treatment of courtship known as 'bruscello' (Jean Canavaggio *Cervantès, dramaturge: Un théâtre à naître*, p. 150).

104 Cervantes also left Italy with recommendations, including one from Don Juan of Austria, which not only did him no good when he was taken prisoner, but were also useless when he finally returned to Spain.

105 The sash was normally worn across the chest, or sometimes around the waist. According to *Autoridades* the colour of the sash was a mark of national identity: hence, Spanish soldiers wore red sashes, the French army wore white and the Dutch wore orange (s.v. 'Banda'). Documents were carried in a metal tube resembling a telescope, also slung across the chest. (See *The Election of the Magistrates of Daganzo*.)

106 A sexton was a lay member of the church, responsible for looking after the building, as well as for digging graves and ringing the bells for the various offices.

107 This passage depends on a complex wordplay: on one level the images refer to a pack of cards, while on another the two men trade accusations of heresy ('Sota-sacristán de Satanás', 'Caballo de Ginebra') (Spadaccini, *Entremeses*, p. 171). See my 'Note on the Translation' for a comment on the translation of this passage.

108 Quince jelly ('carne de membrillo') is a delicacy that can still be enjoyed in Spain. In Cervantes's time it was sold in square boxes made of thin wood, as shown in a painting by the eighteenth-century Spanish painter Luis Meléndez (*Still Life with Oranges and Walnuts*) in the National Gallery, London.

109 The sexton means that his baldness is not the result of the tonsure (i.e. the ritual shaving of the head required of priests and monks). Since he is not yet ordained he is not obliged to be celibate.

110 According to Aesop's fable, the dog-in-the-manger neither eats nor allows anyone else to eat.

111 Although the sexton is a lay person, he has taken the first step towards ordination (cf. note 109).

112 The sexton's name is Pasillas ('little raisins').

113 See note 100.

114 The boy is a 'santero', responsible for soliciting money for the upkeep of a shrine in a hermitage. St Lucy was a Christian martyr at the time of the Emperor Diocletian. She supposedly plucked out her eyes rather than submit to prostitution. For this reason, or because her name derives from the Latin word 'lux', her help is invoked against diseases of the eyes.

115 Goods usually offered for sale by French peddlers, although by his name Manuel is probably Portuguese. Both French and Portuguese men had the reputation of being flirtatious.

116 '. . . señora de los vivos, y aun señora de los muertos': the punning here involves an untranslatable play on two meanings of 'vivo' ('trimming', and 'living'), contrasted with 'muerto' ('dead').

117 The shoemaker's name is Juan Juncos, which translates almost exactly into Jack Straw, with a similar comic connotation. The Calle Mayor was the principal thoroughfare in Madrid in Cervantes's time, well known for its shops and as a place to meet, to stroll and to flirt.

118 Cervantes is poking fun at Lope de Vega as a writer of sonnets.

To claim that something was by Lope was to express unqualified admiration.

119 The soldier suggests that the shoemaker has an intelligence worthy of a student at the Trilingual College in the University of Alcalá (where students studied Greek, Latin and Hebrew).

120 Cervantes himself was familiar with this region of Italy as a soldier in the service of Don Juan of Austria in the 1570s.

120 The soldier uses the expression 'Señor dulce', suggesting that he has an easy time of it.

122 This object was probably used in much the same way as a feather duster. However, a seventeenth-century audience may also have recognised it as a 'matapecados' ('sinbeater'), a stick with strips of leather attached to it, used at the end of many Interludes to administer mock beatings. Eugenio Asensio notes that it was the equivalent of the English 'fool's whip'. A parody of the hyssop, a religious symbol of purification, it often featured in carnivals and Corpus Christi festivities (*Itinerario del entremés*, pp. 21–2).

123 A humorous allusion to the legend of Ursula, the Christian daughter of the king of Brittany, who was martyred by the Huns, along with eleven thousand virgins.

124 Cervantes names a specific cannon ('el de Dio que está en Lisboa'), captured by the Portuguese from the Turks in 1538 in the battle of Diu. Famous for its size, it could still be seen in Lisbon during Cervantes's lifetime.

125 Intellect, will and memory were regarded as the three attributes of the soul.

126 The main bridge leading into Madrid on the north side of the city.

127 The allusion is double: on the one hand it quotes a popular saying 'Por el hilo se saca el ovillo ('the thread will lead you to the ball of yarn') – i.e. one finds out everything eventually; on the other, it refers literally to the threadbare condition of the soldier's clothes. A suitable gesture on the part of the actor can add a ribald touch to the words.

128 The social and historical background to the Interlude is discussed in Carroll B. Johnson, 'Structures and Social Structures in *El vizcaíno fingido*'.

129 The Basque 'squire' whom Don Quixote confronts in I, 8 speaks in similarly garbled fashion. Cervantes notes in his Prologue to the Plays and Interludes that a Biscayan sometimes featured in Lope de Rueda's Interludes (although no such text is known today).

130 Carroll Johnson suggests that perhaps he took her for a lady when she was riding in a coach with her face covered.

131 The practical joke ('burla') was a favourite pastime in seventeenth-century Spain; see for example the elaborate tricks and hoaxes devised by the Duke and Duchess at the expense of Don Quixote and Sancho (*Don Quixote*, II).

132 Nicholas Spadaccini and Jenaro Talens, *Through the Shattering Glass*, p. 44.

133 Carroll Johnson suggests that Brigida's husband is serving a prison term (perhaps as a galley slave).

134 One of the places where public proclamations were made (see *The Divorce Court Judge*).

135 A law proclaimed in Madrid on 3 January 1611, was known as the 'Premática de los coches' (the Coach Law). It was aimed at reforming immoral public behaviour.

136 Cervantes seems to suggest that coaches and galleys share a common characteristic: they both harbour criminals and disreputable people (Johnson pp. 10–11).

137 The law of 1611 expressly forbade owners to lend out their coaches.

138 It was fashionable for ladies to wear voluminous cloaks made of a fine, transparent silk (known as 'mantos de soplillo' because a breath of wind would displace them). 'Chapines' were shoes with high heels built on layers of cork, sometimes trimmed with silver. In 1623 the height of these heels would be limited and the silver trimmings banned together.

139 Brigida actually says that she will dance the 'polvillo', a popular measure condemned by the authorities as immoral; the same dance is mentioned in *The Election of the Magistrates of Daganzo*.

140 Solorzano called himself a 'cortesano', which, in this context, means that he is a citizen of the city in which the king and his court reside (i.e. Madrid).

141 Solórzano is referring to the University of Salamanca, founded in the thirteenth century.

142 The silversmiths' shops were in a section of the Calle Mayor near the Guadalajara Gate.

143 A reference to an episode in Ovid's *Metamorphoses* (Book IV). Pyramus killed himself when he learned of the supposed death of Thisbe, whereupon she also committed suicide.

144 Genoese bankers were long established in Spain and a major influence in the country's economy at the time of Cervantes. In 1611 a royal decree deferred payment of debts owed to these bankers until the arrival of silver from America the following year (Bonilla 219).

145 Frenchmen were reputed to be heavy drinkers.

146 It was a common belief (prompted by moralists and the Church) that the make-up women used on their faces was a cause of ageing, tooth decay and bad breath. In fact, these effects were probably the result of poisoning by lead or mercury in the make-up.

147 A popular saying, sometimes varied as 'ugly women are lucky with husbands'.

148 Collars made of starched lace mounted on hoops were also banned by the sumptuary laws of 1611. Brigida clearly considers her own unembellished appearance to be less deceiving than that of Cristina.

149 Literally: 'he gives you the chain, even though he may not be sleeping here . . .'

150 A legendary Christian emperor thought to have ruled either in the Far East, Ethiopia or Abyssina.

151 Specifically from San Martín de Valdeiglesias, in the region of La Mancha. This wine was very highly regarded in the best circles in Madrid, where it was sometimes called the Saint's wine. The notion that a prostitute would serve an expensive vintage wine is plainly comic.

152 A reference to the transformations experienced by the legendary characters in Ovid's *Metamorphoses*.

153 The amount of money exchanged keeps varying. In all, Cristina pays out ten ducats to Solorzano, six to the constable and anything from one to thirty on the dinner!

154 A popular saying indicating that everything exacts a price in the end.

155 Maurice Molho traces the background and transmission of this folk motif in *Cervantes: raíces folklóricas*, pp. 46–105.

156 'Entremeses'. In *Suma cervantina*, ed. J. B. Avalle-Arce and E. C. Riley (London: Tamesis, 1973), p. 190.

157 Molho, *Cervantes: raíces folklóricas*, p. 164.

158 See N. Spadaccini and J. Talens, *Through the Shattering Glass*, pp. 55–8.

159 *Through the Shattering Glass*, p. 58.

160 This was a popular theme in Spain in the sixteenth and seventeenth centuries. Its best-known expression can be found in a treatise by Fray Antonio de Guevara, published in 1539 with the title *Menosprecio de corte y alabanza de aldea* (*With Scorn for the City and Praise for the Village*).

161 See D. Smith, 'Cervantes and his Audience: Aspects of Reception Theory in *El retablo de las maravillas*'.

162 The names of the characters in this Interlude are all comic, either by suggestion or direct allusion.

CHANFALLA: although no identical word exists, the prefix 'chan' suggests an element of untrustworthiness (Molho, p. 172).

CHIRINOS: (Cherinos in the original 1615 edition) is associated with 'Cherinola', a word meaning 'a gathering of thieves' in the language of the underworld (*Autoridades*).

RABELIN: a diminutive form of 'rabel', a musical instrument resembling a lute with a high, sharp sound. *Autoridades* notes that the word was used to refer jokingly to the buttocks of young boys. Molho also suggests that it meant a child who intrudes between a man and woman.

BENITO REPOLLO/TERESA REPOLLA: Benito and Teresa Cabbage.

JUAN CASTRADO/JUANA CASTRADA: I have opted for the Italian form which is more familiar to English readers.

PEDRO CAPACHO: Peter Fruit Basket.

163 This trick may have originated in a folktale in which a poor student tricks a group of credulous villagers into believing that he is a magician who can make it rain.

164 Rabelin is referring to a type of company that shared the profits among the actors, as opposed to one in which the manager paid the actors a fixed salary and kept the takings for himself (Spadaccini, *Entremeses*, p. 217).

165 'May you never leave it for a better' translates the problematic line 'Con venirlo a ser de las Algarrobillas, los deseche' (see Spadaccini, *Entremeses*, p. 218).

166 Chirinos ridicules the contemporary belief that honour depended on an untainted Christian pedigree, so that even peasants could claim to be 'hombres honrados'.

167 In 1610 there was a shortage of playwrights in Madrid (Spadaccini, *Entremeses*, p. 219). Puppet shows were occasionally presented in the Corrales de Comedias in Madrid (see J. E. Varey, *Historia de los títeres en España* [Madrid: *Revista de Occidente*, 1957], p. 206).

168 Tontonelo is an invented name combining the word 'tonto' ('mad', 'foolish') with the vaguely italianate suffix '-nelo'. I have used the English word 'tomfool', with its connotation of 'a half-witted man'; or, in the usage of the mid-seventeenth century, 'a buffoon who accompanies morris-dancers; . . . a laughing-stock' (*OED*).

169 The prohibition is directed particularly against Jews who had converted to Catholicism ('conversos').

170 *ante omnia* ('before all else'). The Mayor shows his ignorance by mistaking the Latin phrase for the name of a person.

171 Chirinos evidently expresses Cervantes's own sour views about the contemporary theatrical world of Madrid, particularly its domination by Lope de Vega and his followers.

172 These absurd titles are possibly an ironic allusion to the satirical sonnets for which the poet Francisco de Quevedo (1580–1645) was famous.

173 Another name for the Sultan of Constantinople – the great enemy of Spain, in whose decisive defeat at the Battle of Lepanto (1571) Cervantes had played a part.

174 The River Guadalquivir caused several severe floods in Seville during the years when Cervantes was probably writing his Interludes.

175 The 'tapestry' ('repostero') is only a blanket (see the stage direction at the end of the Interlude).

176 This is probably a reference to an actual event (Molho, p. 206).

177 The water from the Jordan River was believed to have the power of rejuvenation.

178 Benito Repollo is characteristically indelicate in claiming that the water has soaked through to his alimentary canal ('canal maestra').

179 Herodias was the wife of King Herod. When the prophet John the Baptist condemned their marriage as unlawful, Herodias had her daughter Salomé dance for her stepfather and tricked him into giving her the head of St John the Baptist as her reward (Matthew 14, 6–10). Cory A. Reed notes that the confusion of mother and daughter was common in medieval and Renaissance Europe (1992:9).

180 Both dances were considered immoral. Their popularity spread to other countries, including England; Queen Elizabeth herself appears in a contemporary picture, kicking up her heels in the saraband. See *The Magic Cave of Salamanca*, and *The Widowed Pimp*, for other references to 'scandalous' dances.

181 A quartermaster ('furrier') was responsible for finding quarters for the army in the towns and villages it passed through. Only those who had documents to prove they were gentlemen ('hidalgos') were exempt from the requirement to provide lodgings.

182 'He's one of them!' Cervantes uses the Latin words 'De ex illis', taken from the story in the Gospels of St Peter's denial of Christ (Matthew 26, 73). The phrase was commonly used to denote Jewish ancestry.

183 According to one version of the legend, the devil himself gave lessons in astrology, magic and the occult sciences to seven students for seven years. Lots were drawn to determine who would pay the teacher and if the payment was not forthcoming, the defaulter would remain a prisoner in the cave for a further seven years. In the fifteenth century one such prisoner supposedly escaped by hiding in a winejar. (Miguel García, 'El tema de la cueva de Salamanca y el entremés cervantino de este título.' *Anales cervantinos* I [1951], pp. 73–109).

184 See the Exemplary Novel called 'The Jealous Extremaduran' (*El celoso extremeño*) for an example of an elderly husband with a young wife who attracts the attention of a would-be suitor. In another Exemplary Novel, 'The Illustrious Kitchen Maid' (*La ilustre fregona*) two students from noble families decide to become 'pícaros'.

185 Cervantes quotes some popular sixteenth-century verses (see Spadaccini [1982, p. 239]).

186 A reference to a ceremony celebrated on Thursday of Holy Week in which the king washed the feet of thirteen beggars, who then received baskets filled with gifts. The hamper is more like an Easter hamper because it contains meat – forbidden during the Lenten season.

187 Students in seventeenth-century Spain usually wore a short tunic and a cloak without a collar.

188 Roque Guinarde was a Catalan bandit famous for his chivalrous conduct. Don Quixote and Sancho encounter his namesake Roque Guinart in *Don Quixote* II, 60.

189 Cristina refers to the army as 'el real' ('the royal one') and plays with the two meanings of 'reliquias' ('relics' and 'leftovers'). She suggests that 'his hunger will be able to worship the relics from the basket' ('. . . habrá en quien adore su hambre').

190 The word 'pelar' in Spanish has a variety of meanings, some of them sexual. 'Pluck' fits most of those meanings, while still remaining ambiguous.

191 The sexton uses the type of pedantic language often ridiculed by Golden Age writers for its latinisms and obscure references. He calls the two women 'automedones', a word created from the name of Achilles' coachman, as found in the *Iliad*.

192 Antonio Nebrija was a fifteenth-century Latin scholar and author of the first Grammar published in Spain, in 1492.

193 The word 'vísperas' means both Vespers and the eve of some event, hence the sexton's uneasy reaction.

194 The Spanish text is a paraphrase of St Paul's famous words on the subject of charity (I Corinthians 13, 8).

195 Lucrecia and Portia were two Roman heroines famous for their faithfulness and chastity.

196 Charcoal was commonly used for heating and cooking in seventeenth-century Spain (see *The Divorce Court Judge*, note 35).

197 The student hints at his familiarity with magic arts and Pancracio rises to the bait. Cararraolano seems to mean that if he were free to

practise his magic powers he would spend his fortune on himself, rather than leaving it to his heirs.

198 Critics have pointed out that these verses are a parody of a passage in *El laberinto de Fortuna*, by the fifteenth-century poet Juan de Mena.

199 The allusion is to a Spanish proverb: 'El perro del herrero duerme a las martilladas y despierta a las dentelladas' ('The blacksmith's dog sleeps through hammer blows but is awakened by the sounds of chewing').

200 See note 85.

201 Compare this with the line in *The Man who Pretended to be from Biscay*, in which Solorzano assures his friend Quiñones that the trick he plans to play on Doña Cristina 'won't offend God or harm anyone'. Cervantes seems anxious to emphasise the relative harmlessness of the hoaxes which are at the centre of these Interludes.

202 The song appears to be ridiculing professors at the University of Salamanca: in particular the lines translated as 'those who teach there ... An arsenal of blackest arts.' The original reads:

> Siéntanse los que alli enseñan
> De alquitrán en una banca,
> Porque estas bombas encierra
> BARBERO: *La Cueva de Salamanca.* [p. 253]

Dr Agustín de la Granja has suggested that 'alquitrán' refers to the dark, resinous oil that was burned in lamps of the type used by scholars. The word 'bomba' has a double meaning, referring both to the bowl of the lamp and to an explosive weapon.

203 See the Introduction for comments on 'scandalous dances'. The Escarramán was a dance named for the legendary picaresque hero featured in *The Widowed Pimp*.

204 *Un Théâtre à Naître*, pp. 213–14.

205 This account is in Allardyce Nicoll, *The World of Harlequin: A Critical Study of the Commedia dell'Arte* (Cambridge: Cambridge University Press, 1963), pp. 10–12. Eduardo Urbina discusses other possible Spanish sources in 'Hacia *El viejo celoso* de Cervantes'. *Nueva Revista de Filología Hispánica*, 38 (1990), pp. 733-42.

206 For a description of the discussion surrounding the two versions,

see *Two Cervantes Short Novels: 'El curioso impertinente' and 'El celoso extremeño*, ed. Frank Pierce (Oxford: Pergamon Press, 1970), p. 24 note 21.

207 Melveena McKendrick believes the Cervantes may have intended this Interlude to be performed together with *Pedro de Urdemalas* on Midsummer's Day (the Feast of St John), to which both plays refer (*Cervantes*, pp. 257–8).

208 Lorenza takes care not to curse the crosses engraved on the coins.

209 Argus was a giant with a hundred eyes set to guard the nymph Io. He was tricked by Hermes, who first lulled him to sleep and then killed him.

210 This verse parodies a popular medieval ballad in which a young woman laments that she has been deceived and abandoned by the knight Gómez Arias (see Edward M. Wilson and J. Sage, *Poesías liricas en las obras dramáticas de Calderón* [London: Tamesis Books, 1964], pp. 146–7).

211 The quotation is from Corinthians 7, 9.

212 Tapestries made of gilded or embossed leather ('guadamecíes') were popular as wall hangings, both in Spain and other parts of Europe in the seventeenth century. The figures which appear on this particular tapestry are all familiar characters from Ludovico Ariosto's epic poem *Orlando Furioso*.

213 Ortigosa means Methuselah, the biblical patriarch who allegedly lived for nine hundred and sixty-nine years (Genesis 5, 27).

214 Cervantes is playing on two meanings of the word 'madre' ('mother' and 'womb'). 'Mal de madre' was the name given to menstrual pains, but also implied an excess of sexual desire or its frustration. Toothache had similar implications as a sexual metaphor (see Javier Herrero on imagery in *La Celestina*, in *Literature among Discourses*, ed. Wlad Godzich and Nicholas Spadaccini [Minneapolis: University of Minnesota Press, 1986], pp. 136–141).

215 The Feast of St John the Baptist falls on 24 June, which is also Midsummer's Day. The idea that quarrels that occur in June are forgotten for the rest of the year also appears in the verses that close *The Divorce Court Judge*.

Despite Cervantes's wish, expressed in the Prologue, that his Plays and Interludes might be 'the best in the world – or, at least, reasonably good', it seems that throughout the seventeenth century they found favour neither on stage nor among the reading public. After their first appearance in print in 1615, more than a century passed before a new edition was published. This was in 1749, at the instigation of the king's librarian Blas Nasarre, whose chief interest in Cervantes's plays seems to have been his desire to attack Lope de Vega as a playwright. (Curiously enough, Nasarre also brought out a new edition of Avellaneda's spurious Second Part of *Don Quixote*, claiming that it was superior to the original!)

In the Prologue to the edition, Nasarre contends that Cervantes deliberately wrote bad plays in order to parody the style of theatre popularised by Lope de Vega:

> [Cervantes] intended that . . . these eight plays and interludes (like so many Don Quixotes and Sanchos, who drove out the portentous and foolish books of chivalry which affected the judgement of many readers) . . . would correct the errors of plays [inspired by Lope] and purge the theatre of bad taste and morals, returning it to the state of reason and normality from which it had strayed in order to please the wretched mob, without respect for the other – more healthy – sector of the public. This revelation did not suit the actors and theatre-managers, well-satisfied with the earnings from their rhymes and verses, so they suppressed this book and did not deign to perform one play from it . . .

Nasarre explains that the satire is more carefully hidden in the plays than in *Don Quixote* because Cervantes could not afford to antagonise the popular playwrights or their public:

> . . . he made do with the Socratic method and with a fine irony which makes clear his opinions and feelings, thus avoiding con-

frontation and a fight with the public and leaving for posterity a testimony of his true desire to oppose disorder.

The collection [of plays] is so grotesque that it does not seem possible that it came from the mind of a sane man. However one may judge Cervantes's plays, no one who reads them in good faith and who reads the prologue (in which their immortal author complains so bitterly that he cannot find actors to perform them, and that only with difficulty can he persuade a bookseller to publish them) will doubt for one moment that they were written in all seriousness.

(Quoted by Armando Cotarelo y Valledor, *El teatro de Cervantes* [Madrid, 1915], pp. 98–990.)

In the battle between the detractors of Golden Age *Comedia* and its defenders, Cervantes's Plays and Interludes became innocent pawns. Leandro Fernández de Moratín, the greatest Spanish playwright of his day, reacted angrily to Nasarre's attack on Lope and his followers by denigrating Cervantes:

So it was that Miguel de Cervantes turned to the theatre, but far from helping to improve it, as he might well have done, he only concerned himself with using it as a means of easing his habitual poverty; he wrote like all the rest and forgot what he knew in order to satisfy the taste of the ordinary public and to win its approval.

(*Discurso histórico sobre los orígenes del teatro*, in *Obras de Don Nicolás y Don Leandro Fernández de Moratín*, Biblioteca de Autores Espǎnoles II [Madrid, 1944], p. 177.)

Another critic dismissed Cervantes's plays as 'so foolish that it seems impossible that so great a genius should have created them': Pedro Estala, *Discurso sobre la comedia antigua y moderna* (Madrid, 1794).

In his *Discurso crítico sobre el origen, calidad y estado presente de las comedias de España* (Madrid, 1750), the lawyer-critic Tomás de Erauso y Zabaleta (using the pseudonym 'A wise man from this Court' [Un ingenio de esta Corte]) launched a similar attack on Cervantes's ability to write plays:

It is a fact that Cervantes's style is inferior to what is customary today: one cannot read his plays without experiencing discomfort in one's ears, and even in one's mind.

Far from believing that Cervantes wrote his plays as a deliberate attack on Lope de Vega, Erauso contends that he was simply a bad playwright:

> ... his creations are poor in appearance and are presented with a definite lack of skill. They have none of the art and spontaneity that please both mind and taste, which always prefer (and rightly so) what is unusual.

(Quoted from Armando Cotarelo y Valledor, *El teatro de Cervantes*, p. 102.)

Part of the ambivalent attitude of Spanish eighteenth-century critics towards Cervantes's plays is explained by the apparent divergence between these plays and the seventeenth-century *Comedia* as represented by Lope de Vega and his followers. Critics were also puzzled by what they believed to be an unaccountable contrast between Cervantes as playwright and Cervantes as author of *Don Quixote* and *The Exemplary Novels*. The Jesuit writer, Francisco Javier Lampillas, offered an ingenious solution: Cervantes was not the true author of the plays, which, according to Lampillas, 'bore the characteristics of an unbalanced mind and warped imagination'.

> I believe that the printers, acting out of malice, used Cervantes's name and his Prologue to publish these grotesque plays, in keeping with the perverted taste of the mob; they either suppressed the ones that were really his, or they changed them completely.

(Quoted in Cotarelo y Valledor, *El teatro de Cervantes*, p. 107.)

Throughout these debates, which had more to do with current views on classicism than with the literary merits of the works in question, Cervantes's Interludes were usually included in the general condemnation of his plays. It was not until 1816 that the Interludes were published separately and, thereafter, acquired a life and reputation of their own. José Cavaleri y Pazos, the editor of the 1816 edition, noted in his introduction that Cervantes was 'gifted with a high degree of comic talent'. In 1826, another critic (Agustín García de Arrieta) claimed that the Interludes occupied third place in the canon of Cervantes's work (after *Don Quixote* and *The Exemplary Novels*).

Nevertheless, throughout Europe in the nineteenth century

Cervantes was principally celebrated as the author of *Don Quixote*. The book was especially popular in Germany, where writers such as Schlegel, Tieck, Heine and Thomas Mann interpreted it according to the ideals of German Romanticism. In Spain, as well, it became fashionable to look for profound allegorical and symbolic meaning in *Don Quixote*. As Anthony Close observes in his study of the reception of *Don Quixote* since 1800 (*The Romantic Approach to 'Don Quixote'*, Cambridge, 1977), Cervantes was scarcely appreciated as a comic writer during this period. The tendency to consider him as a philosophical writer with a high moral purpose may help to explain why his theatre has been so neglected and misunderstood until our own time.

While the Interludes have fared better than the plays, they have also been eclipsed by Cervantes's better-known work in prose. When they found favour in France during the nineteenth century, it was chiefly because they were found to resemble scenes in plays by Molière (who may, incidentally, have known the Interludes and been influenced by them).

The twentieth century has finally brought recognition for the Interludes in their own right and most critics concede that Cervantes transformed the genre and became its greatest exponent. The American hispanist George Ticknor had already noted in 1879:

> The Eight Entremeses are better than the eight full-length plays. They are short farces, generally in prose, with a slight plot, and sometimes with none, and were intended merely to amuse an audience in the intervals between the acts of the longer pieces ... All, indeed, have an air of truth and reality, which, whether they were founded in fact or not, it was evidently the author's purpose to give them.

(From *History of Spanish Literature* II [Boston, 1879], p. 151.)

In their carefully annotated six-volume edition of the Plays and Interludes, published in 1922, Rudolph Schevill and Adolfo Bonilla argue that, despite Cervantes's lack of aptitude as a dramatist, his plays

> do not deserve the neglect and scorn that they have received. Our interest for Cervantes's plays does not – as some believe – derive from the fact that they come from the author of the *Quixote*, but

rather because they represent an advance with respect to the drama that preceded them (Vol. VI, p. 26).

These editors single out for praise:

The artistic value of Cervantes's prose, the ingenuity of his dialogue, his power of invention, his admirable portrayal of *souls* and *bodies* [which] can be appreciated in his greatest creations, of which the Interludes are a precious, but small, part ... There are characters in these Interludes that are equal to any portrayed in the *Quixote* [pp. 157–8].

In 1941 the distinguished Spanish scholar Menéndez Pelayo commented that 'as far as prose interludes are concerned, Cervantes must be given the prize'; in 1951 the English hispanophile Gerald Brenan dismissed Cervantes's plays, but added in a footnote '[his] *Entremeses* ... continuing the tradition of Lope de Rueda's *pasos*, are, however, brilliant' (*The Literature of the Spanish People*, London, 1951, p. 170). The French scholar Robert Marrast characterised the Interludes as 'free theatre' ('théâtre en liberté'),

because in these short pieces Cervantes is concerned neither with political nor religious improvement, nor with aesthetic problems, for the framework offers him quite a lot of flexibility and lends itself to every situation ... Gradually this rudimentary genre begins to transform itself – in Cervantes's writing – until it becomes a comedy of manners in miniature.

(From *Miguel de Cervantès: dramaturge* [Paris, 1957], pp. 114–115.)

In a study of Cervantes's theatre published in 1966, the renowned Cervantes scholar Joaquín Casalduero commented on the originality of Cervantes's comic vision in the Interludes:

It is curious how [Cervantes] eschews comic devices that rely on physical effects – falls, blows, hunger, thirst – all sure audience pleasers, which he himself used in the novel and in his plays. Nor does he make use of social comedy. His comic vision focuses on human nature ... what is important is not the hoax or deception (another traditional means of provoking laughter), but rather the foolishness of man ... Without becoming sentimental or banal,

Cervantes is capable of so much tenderness and generosity that in portraying human folly he is filled with the greatest compassion.

(From *Sentido y forma del teatro de Cervantes* [Madrid 1966], p. 24.)

Casalduero was also among the first critics to praise Cervantes's plays for their dramatic qualities:

> Cervantes published his plays, not because they were successful, but because no one wanted to perform them. He refused to accept the verdict of the actors and theatre-managers. Who knows whether they have come down to us because they were never performed! Cervantes's plays should be read with the respect due to the author, but they have not survived just because they are his [p. 26].

Another outstanding Spanish scholar who did much to draw attention to Cervantes's Interludes was Eugenio Asensio. He concluded that, in spite of Cervantes's originality and daring experimentation in the genre, he did not leave his mark on those who followed him:

> Surprising as it may seem, [they] were moving towards goals that were very different from his: towards a stylised distortion of the characters, towards a clever style of wit, towards a single, explosive effect; but in return, they abandoned as unwanted ballast the harmonious matching of character and situation, the careful observation and the mature reflexion that Cervantes hides behind his comedy.

(From *El itinerario del Entremés* [Madrid, 1965], p. 110.)

In his introduction to a translation of the Interludes in 1964, the American scholar Edwin Honig marvels at Cervantes's ability to create in them what he fails to achieve elsewhere in his writing:

> These eight short plays are among the most beguiling things Cervantes ever wrote. Part of their charm is the appropriateness of the simple dramatic form to Cervantes' lighthearted often elusive treatment of his subjects. This is notable in a writer whose ingenuity in creating character was offset by his casual use of literary forms. Except for *The Siege of Numantia*, his plays read like episodic narratives, his stories like dialogues and dramatic

sketches, and his best-known novel is a hodge-podge of tall tales and long-winded colloquies from which his main characters are often excluded. His pastoral novels, *La Galatea* and *Persiles y Sigismunda*, written according to anachronistic formulas, fail badly; his poetry is often blank verse or a kind of rhymed prose. And when he hastily completed Part II of *Don Quixote*, he did so in self-protection because a literary opportunist named Avellaneda, whom nobody has yet identified, had had the gall to write and publish a fraudulent sequel to the widely popular Part I.

(From 'On the *Interludes* of Cervantes', cited in *Cervantes: A collection of Critical Essays*, ed. Lowry Nelson [Englewood Cliffs: Prentice-Hall, 1969, p. 152].)

Other critics subscribe to the view that Cervantes was unsuccessful in the theatre because he succeeded too well as a novelist. Thus the Spanish poet, José Bergamín, wrote in 1959: 'Cervantes theatricalised the novel because he was unable to novelise the theatre as much and as well as Lope de Vega.' (Quoted in the Introduction to *Miguel de Cervantes: Teatro completo*, ed. Florencio Sevilla Arroyo and Antonio Rey Hazas [Madrid, 1987], p. xxix.)

The editors of this most recent collection of Cervantes's dramatic works themselves endorse this view:

Since the *Eight Plays* could not be performed [in Cervantes's lifetime], and because he was first and foremost a writer of novels, he sometimes directs his stage directions exclusively to the readers of these plays, without taking into account the audience of a possible performance (xxix).

The idea that the Interludes are better read than performed is also expressed by Stanislav Zimic, Professor of Spanish Golden Age Literature at the University of Texas at Austin, in a recent study of Cervantes's theatre, *El teatro de Cervantes* [Madrid, 1992], p. 403):

In accordance with Cervantes's own views, we see that the merits of his plays are mainly literary ones: they can only be properly appreciated if they are read. Paradoxically, however, it is through reading them that we become aware of the importance of Cervantes's plays in the history and theory of Golden Age drama. They clearly attempt to bring about radical, unprecedented innovations in dramatic conception and theatrical presentation, not to mention their often brilliant ideas in staging. Through reading them we become aware that, taken as a whole, Cervantes's plays are a daring and revolutionary theatrical experiment ... They represent a fascinating chapter that cannot be overlooked if we are to reach a clear understanding, not only of Cervantes, but also of Spanish Golden Age culture as a whole.

This apparent paradox has become central to current critical discussion of Cervantes's contribution as a playwright. Nicholas Spadaccini, Professor of Comparative Literature at the University of Minnesota, goes so far as to claim that 'in 1615, [Cervantes] opts to publish his dramatic works instead of turning them over to theatrical producers' (p. 52). In an essay entitled 'Writing for Reading: Cervantes's Aesthetics of Reception in the *Entremeses*', in *Critical Essays on Cervantes*, ed. Ruth El Saffar (Boston, 1986), pp. 162–75, Spadaccini argues that:

The private reception through reading allows Cervantes to circumvent the possibility of a closed canon. That is, while closure is achieved in an *entremés* within the framework of a staged performance, with the private sphere of reading there occurs a textualization which virtually excludes that possibility ... [T]he private reading of those comic pieces allows for a reception that is potentially demystifying and subversive [p. 166].

In *Through the Shattering Glass: Cervantes and the Self-Made World* (Minneapolis, 1993), Spadaccini and co-author Jenaro Talens (Professor of Spanish Literature and of Literary Theory and Film at the University of Valencia) carry this argument further:

Cervantes's *entremeses* are defined by their dialogical relationship with the new art of writing and producing plays that is institutionalized in Spain at the beginning of the 1600s under Lope de Vega's theoretical-ideological impulse. Vis-à-vis that theatre, which tends to reflect social myths, and 'in which the established reality is supported ideologically' (Maravall), Cervantes's *entremeses* opt for a critical and demystifying attitude toward prevailing and official ideologies. In these comic pieces or plays of 'low style', the observations of the artist and those of the discriminating receiver of his product are directed toward those vital and social areas that are rarely explored by the so-called new comedy of the early 1600s. We might also say that it is precisely the opposition between reading, on the one hand, and the witnessing of a staged performance, on the other, that provokes in Cervantes's discourse the necessity to inscribe the 'stage' in the written page, that is, to transform theatricality into narrativity [p. 63].

Cory A. Reed's study of Cervantes's Interludes, *The Novelist as Playwright: Cervantes and the 'Entremés nuevo'* (New York, 1993) also stresses the narrative influence in the Interludes:

In short, Cervantes fuses the popular, theatrical form of the traditional *entremés* and the more thematically profound composition of character and plot found in prose narrative. His characters are more complex and individualized, his situations suggest possible psychological interpretations, and his thematic content invites socio-historical analysis. Such intricacies, common in twentieth-century short drama, but typically characteristic of prose literature in Cervantes's time, were entirely absent from the conventional *entremés* performed between the acts of the *comedia* [pp. 15–16].

Reed, however, also concedes that Cervantes 'did not fail because of any lack of theatricality' (p. 188).

A more balanced view of Cervantes's achievements as a playwright is offered by Edward H. Friedman, Professor of Spanish at the University of Indiana, in *The Unifying Concept: Approaches to the Structure of Cervantes' Comedias* (1981), p. 15.

Cervantes wrote no literary treatises as such, but statements within his works reveal a preoccupation with method and organization of material ... Two factors delineate Cervantes' venture into drama: his intense desire to succeed as a playwright and his ultimate rejection by a public indoctrinated in Lope's *comedia*. Relative acceptance of the early plays wanes as Lope triumphs, and Cervantes' bitterness is understandable and unconcealed. It seems apparent from his references to drama that Cervantes believed in the intrinsic quality of his plays, demonstrating a characteristic self-confidence and forcefulness in moments of adversity. At a time when no theatrical manager would buy his plays, Cervantes left the final judgement to future critics by selling the *comedias* and *entremeses* to a bookseller who offered to publish them.

While most of the critics cited in this survey have preferred to judge Cervantes's plays as literary artefacts, there are a few who contend that Cervantes was ahead of his time as a playwright. Jean Canavaggio, Professor of French Literature at the Université de Caen, gave his 1977 study of Cervantes's theatre the title *Un Théâtre à Naître* (Paris, 1977). His comment in the preface seems aptly prescient:

'Theatre that misses the mark' ['un théâtre manqué']: by characterising Cervantes's output as a playwright in this way, critics have unequivocally confirmed the judgement of posterity. It would be absurd to answer that judgement retrospectively; however, aside from the fact that history never changes its views, it would also be wrong to treat it as unchangeable. We have not been given a verdict without appeal; this opinion is merely relative and must be judged by taking into consideration . . . the circumstances of its origin (11).

In recent years, the Compañía Nacional de Teatro Clásico in Madrid has staged very successful productions of *Los Baños de Argel* (*The Bagnios of Algiers*) and *La Gran Sultana* (*The Grand Sultana*).

Francisco Nieva, the director of *The Bagnios of Algiers*, wrote of his experience:

Whoever looks seriously at Cervantes's plays from a modern perspective, naturally sees many [. . .] things. [. . .] One sees something that predates romanticism and leans towards melodrama. One sees a structure open to visual possibilities (a feature of Cervantine drama that is usually ignored). This is an infuriating and total theatre which demands the full collaboration of music, song, dance and visual elements. The proposition is almost Wagnerian. One might even say worthy of Fellini.

(From 'Teatro clásico español: problemas de una lectura actual', in *II Jornadas de Teatro Clásico Español* [Almagro, 1979], p. 198.)

Outside Spain the Interludes have had an influence on writers as diverse as A. N. Ostrovsky in Russia, Bertolt Brecht in Germany and Jacques Prévert in France. In the 1930s Federico

García Lorca revived *Sir Vigilant* and *The Magic Cave of Salamanca* as part of the repertoire of his travelling student company known as La Barraca. The success of the Interludes on the stage is, perhaps, best illustrated by a brief account by Lorca's friend José María Salaverría of a performance of *Sir Vigilant* given by Federico García Lorca and his company of itinerant actors in 1932. After noting that while the company performed Calderón de la Barca to urban audiences, it chose simpler plays for rural audiences, he continues:

> It seems that Cervantes's Interlude *Sir Vigilant* met with repeated success. In spite of the anachronistic language and the unfamiliarity of the characters and subjects, the public followed with great curiosity the unfolding of that fictive creation which has preserved through the centuries the true flavour of its origin and the eternal mark of genius.

(Quoted in *Federico García Lorca: obras completas* [Madrid, 1963] p. 1711.)

SUGGESTIONS FOR FURTHER READING

For background reading on Cervantes and his times:

Fernand Braudel, *The Mediterranean and the Mediterranean World in the Age of Philip II*, 2 vols., tr. from the French by Sian Reynolds (London: Collins, 1973).

Jean Canavaggio, *Cervantes*, tr. from the French by J. R. Jones (New York: W. W. Norton, 1990).

J. H. Elliott, 'Monarchy and Empire (1474–1700)', in *Spain: A Companion to Spanish Studies*, ed. P. E. Russell (London: Methuen, 1973), pp. 107–144.

Henry Kamen, *Inquisition and Society in Spain in the Sixteenth and Seventeenth Centuries* (London: Weidenfeld and Nicolson, 1985).

John Lynch, *Spain under the Habsburgs*, 2 vols. (Oxford: Basil Blackwell, 1965 and 1969).

José Antonio Maravall, *Culture of the Baroque*, tr. Terry Cochrane (Minneapolis: University of Minnesota Press, 1986).

Melveena McKendrick, *Cervantes* (Boston: Little, Brown, 1980).

Geoffrey Parker, *Philip II* (London: Hutchinson, 1978).

For general background on the theatre in Cervantes's time and for specific studies of his *Interludes*:

Jean Canavaggio, *Cervantès dramaturge: Un théâtre à naître* (Paris: Presses Universitaires de France, 1977).

Edward H. Friedman, *The Unifying Concept: Approaches to the Structure of Cervantes' 'Comedias'* (York, South Carolina: Spanish Literature Publications Company, 1981).

Jean Graham-Jones, ' "Tuya soy": the Economics of Marriage in Cervantes's *Entremés del rufián viudo llamado Trampagos*', in *Bulletin of the Comediantes*, 44, (1992), pp. 151–61.

Carroll B. Johnson, 'Structures and Social Structures in *El vizcaíno fingido*', in *Bulletin of the Comediantes*, 41, (1989), pp. 7–20.

Melveena McKendrick, *Theatre in Spain, 1490–1700* (Cambridge: Cambridge University Press, 1989).

Mary Gaylord Randel, 'The Order in the Court: Cervantes' *Entremés del juez de los divorcios*', in *Bulletin of the Comediantes*, 34, (1982), pp. 83–95.

Cory A. Reed, 'Dirty Dancing: Salome, Herodias and *El retablo de las maravillas*', in *Bulletin of the Comediantes*, 44, (1992), pp. 7–20.

Cory A. Reed, *The Novelist as Playwright: Cervantes and the 'Entremés nuevo'* (New York: Peter Lang, 1993).

Michael K. Schuessler, 'Textualization of Tradition: *El vizcaíno fingido* and the Development of the *Entremés* as a Literary Genre', in *Bulletin of the Comediantes*, 44, (1992), pp. 231–41.

N. D. Shergold, *A History of the Spanish Stage from Medieval Times until the End of the Seventeenth Century* (Oxford: Clarendon Press, 1967).

Dawn L. Smith, 'Cervantes and his Audience: Aspects of Reception Theory in *El retablo de las maravillas*', in *The Golden Age Comedia: Text, Theory and Performance*, ed. Charles Ganelin and Howard Mencing (West Lafayette: Purdue University Press, 1994), pp. 249–61.

Nicholas Spadaccini, 'Writing for Reading: Cervantes's Aesthetics of Reception in the *Entremeses*', in *Critical Essays on Cervantes*, ed. Ruth El Saffar (Boston: G. K. Hall, 1986), pp. 162–75.

Nicholas Spadaccini with Jenaro Talens, *Through the Shattering Glass: Cervantes and the Self-Made World* (Minneapolis: University of Minnesota Press, 1993).

Stanislav Zimic, *El teatro de Cervantes* (Madrid: Castalia, 1992).

Other Works by Cervantes

(In English translation)

Don Quixote tr. J. M. Cohen (London: Penguin Books, 1950).
Exemplary Novels ed. B. W. Ife, 4 vols. (Warminster: Aris and Phillips, 1992).

ACKNOWLEDGEMENTS

I am grateful to my colleagues, friends, students and family for their advice and encouragement during the preparation of this volume. I wish to express my special appreciation to Ellen Anderson, Don Beecher, Douglas Campbell, Agustín de la Granja and Melveena McKendrick for their sound comments and suggestions. Trent University made funds available for secretarial assistance and Tina Merchant helped with preparing the manuscript. My greatest debt is to María Luz Valencia, who helped guide the project through many years of gestation. Her fluent appreciation of both languages and her wise comments on every draft of the translation added immeasurably to the pleasure of the undertaking. My husband Denis, as always, was a patient and appreciative reader and an unfailingly helpful critic.

DRAMA
IN EVERYMAN

The Oresteia
AESCHYLUS
New translation of one of the greatest Greek dramatic trilogies which analyses the plays in performance
£5.99

Everyman and Medieval Miracle Plays
edited by A. C. Cawley
A selection of the most popular medieval plays
£4.99

Complete Plays and Poems
CHRISTOPHER MARLOWE
The complete works of this great Elizabethan in one volume
£5.99

Restoration Plays
edited by Robert Lawrence
Five comedies and two tragedies representing the best of the Restoration stage
£7.99

Female Playwrights of the Restoration: Five Comedies
edited by Paddy Lyons
Rediscovered literary treasures in a unique selection
£5.99

Plays, Prose Writings and Poems
OSCAR WILDE
The full force of Wilde's wit in one volume
£4.99

A Dolls House/The Lady from the Sea/The Wild Duck
HENRIK IBSEN
introduced by Fay Weldon
A popular selection of Ibsen's major plays
£4.99

The Beggar's Opera and Other Eighteenth-Century Plays
JOHN GAY et. al.
Including Goldsmith's She Stoops To Conquer *and Sheridan's* The School for Scandal, *this is a volume which reflects the full scope of the period's theatre*
£6.99

Female Playwrights of the Nineteenth Century
edited by Adrienne Scullion
The full range of female nineteenth-century dramatic development
£6.99

All books are available from your local bookshop or direct from:
Littlehampton Book Services Cash Sales, 14 Eldon Way, Lineside Estate,
Littlehampton, West Sussex BN17 7HE (*prices are subject to change*)

To order any of the books, please enclose a cheque (in sterling) made payable to
Littlehampton Book Services, or phone your order through with credit card details (Access,
Visa or Mastercard) on 01903 721596 (24 hour answering service) stating card number
and expiry date. (*Please add £1.25 for package and postage to the total of your order.*)

In the USA, for further information and a complete catalogue call 1-800-526-2778

FOREIGN LITERATURE IN TRANSLATION IN EVERYMAN

A Hero of Our Time
MIKHAIL LERMONTOV
The Byronic adventures of a Russian army officer
£5.99

L'Assommoir
ÉMILE ZOLA
One of the most successful novels of the nineteenth century and one of the most scandalous
£6.99

Poor Folk and The Gambler
FYODOR DOSTOYEVSKY
These two short works of doomed passion are among Dostoyevsky's quintessential best. Combination unique to Everyman
£4.99

Yevgeny Onegin
ALEXANDER PUSHKIN
Pushkin's novel in verse is Russia's best-loved literary work. It contains some of the loveliest Russian poetry ever written
£5.99

The Three-Cornered Hat
ANTONIO PEDRO DE ALARCÓN
A rollicking farce and one of the world's greatest masterpieces of humour. Available only in Everyman
£4.99

Notes from Underground and A Confession
FYODOR DOSTOYEVSKY *and* LEV TOLSTOY
Russia's greatest novelists ruthlessly tackle the subject of their mid-life crises. Combination unique to Everyman
£4.99

Selected Stories
ANTON CHEKHOV
edited and revised by Donald Rayfield
Masterpieces of compression and precision. Selection unique to Everyman
£7.99

Selected Writings
VOLTAIRE
A comprehensive edition of Voltaire's best writings. Selection unique to Everyman
£6.99

Fontamara
IGNAZIO SILONE
'A beautifully composed tragedy. Fontamara is as fresh now, and as moving, as it must have been when first published.' London Standard. Available only in Everyman
£4.99

All books are available from your local bookshop or direct from:
Littlehampton Book Services Cash Sales, 14 Eldon Way, Lineside Estate, Littlehampton, West Sussex BN17 7HE (*prices are subject to change*)

To order any of the books, please enclose a cheque (in sterling) made payable to *Littlehampton Book Services*, or phone your order through with credit card details (Access, Visa or Mastercard) on 01903 721596 (24 hour answering service) stating card number and expiry date. (*Please add £1.25 for package and postage to the total of your order.*)

In the USA, for further information and a complete catalogue call 1-800-526-2778

CLASSIC NOVELS
IN EVERYMAN

The Time Machine
H. G. WELLS

One of the books which defined
'science fiction' – a compelling
and tragic story of a brilliant
and driven scientist
£3.99

Oliver Twist
CHARLES DICKENS

Arguably the best-loved of
Dickens's novels. With all the
original illustrations
£4.99

Barchester Towers
ANTHONY TROLLOPE

The second of Trollope's
Chronicles of Barsetshire,
and one of the funniest of all
Victorian novels
£4.99

The Heart of Darkness
JOSEPH CONRAD

Conrad's most intense, subtle,
compressed, profound and
proleptic work
£3.99

Tess of the d'Urbervilles
THOMAS HARDY

The powerful, poetic classic
of wronged innocence
£3.99

Wuthering Heights and Poems
EMILY BRONTË

A powerful work of genius – one of
the great masterpieces of literature
£3.99

Pride and Prejudice
JANE AUSTEN

Proposals, rejections, infidelities,
elopements, happy marriages –
Jane Austen's most popular novel
£2.99

North and South
ELIZABETH GASKELL

A novel of hardship, passion
and hard-won wisdom amidst the
conflicts of the industrial revolution
£4.99

The Newcomes
W. M. THACKERAY

An exposé of Victorian polite
society by one of the nineteenth-
century's finest novelists
£6.99

Adam Bede
GEORGE ELIOT

A passionate rural drama enacted
at the turn of the eighteenth
century
£5.99

All books are available from your local bookshop or direct from:
Littlehampton Book Services Cash Sales, 14 Eldon Way, Lineside Estate,
Littlehampton, West Sussex BN17 7HE (*prices are subject to change*)

To order any of the books, please enclose a cheque (in sterling) made payable to
Littlehampton Book Services, or phone your order through with credit card details (Access,
Visa or Mastercard) on 01903 721596 (24 hour answering service) stating card number
and expiry date. (*Please add £1.25 for package and postage to the total of your order.*)

In the USA, for further information and a complete catalogue call 1-800-526-2778

SHAKESPEARE
IN EVERYMAN

*Edited by John Andrews, the Everyman Shakespeare is the
most comprehensive, up-to-date paperback edition of
the plays and poems, featuring:*

face-to-face text and notes

chronology of Shakespeare's life and times

a rich selection of **critical and theatrical responses**
to the play over the centuries

foreword by an actor or director describing
the play in performance

up-to-date commentary on the play

Antony and Cleopatra £3.99

Hamlet £2.99

Julius Caesar £3.99

King Lear £2.99

Macbeth £2.99

Measure for Measure £3.99

The Merchant of Venice £2.99

A Midsummer Night's Dream
£1.99

Othello £3.99

Romeo and Juliet £2.99

The Tempest £2.99

Twelfth Night £3.99

The Winter's Tale £3.99

All books are available from your local bookshop or direct from:
Littlehampton Book Services Cash Sales, 14 Eldon Way, Lineside Estate,
Littlehampton, West Sussex BN17 7HE *(prices are subject to change)*

To order any of the books, please enclose a cheque (in sterling) made payable to
Littlehampton Book Services, or phone your order through with credit card details (Access,
Visa or Mastercard) on 01903 721596 (24 hour answering service) stating card number
and expiry date. *(Please add £1.25 for package and postage to the total of your order.)*

In the USA, for further information and a complete catalogue call 1-800-526-2778